Second Edition

Summertime Learning

Prepare Your Child for Seventh Grade

Editorial Project Manager
Eric Migliaccio

Editor in Chief
Brent L. Fox, M. Ed.

Creative Director
Sarah M. Fournier

Cover Artist
Diem Pascarella

Illustrator
Clint McKnight

Art Coordinator
Renée Mc Elwee

Imaging
Amanda R. Harter

Publisher
Mary D. Smith, M.S. Ed.

Teacher Created Resources
12621 Western Avenue
Garden Grove, CA 92841
www.teachercreated.com

ISBN: 978-1-4206-8847-4

©2022 Teacher Created Resources
Reprinted, 2022

Made in U.S.A.

Teacher Created Resources

Table of Contents

An Important Message from the National Summer Learning Association 4

Using This Book 5

Weekly Calendar 7

Journal Topics 8

Standards and Skills 9

Week 1 Activities

Monday   *Math:* Products & Quotients — *Reading:* Nine Brains, No Bones 12

Tuesday   *Science:* Earth's Layers — *Writing:* Run-On Sentences 14

Wednesday   *Math:* Time and Distance — *Reading:* Fact or Opinion? 16

Thursday   *Writing:* Sensory Words — *Social Studies:* Where in the World? 18

Friday   *Testing:* Complete Sentences — *Friday Fun:* Magic Math 20

Week 2 Activities

Monday   *Math:* Liquid Measurement — *Writing:* Phrases & Clauses 22

Tuesday   *Reading:* Story Sequence — *Social Studies:* Mummies 24

Wednesday   *Math:* Fraction Frenzy — *Writing:* Can You Elaborate? 26

Thursday   *Science:* More Than Planets — *Reading:* Big Foot Vocabulary 28

Friday   *Testing:* Multiply & Divide Fractions — *Friday Fun:* Rhyming Riddles 30

Week 3 Activities

Monday   *Math:* Decimals Crossword — *Reading:* Nelson Mandela 32

Tuesday   *Science:* Inherited Traits — *Writing:* Quotation Marks 34

Wednesday   *Math:* Interest in Banking — *Reading:* Vocabulary Practice 36

Thursday   *Writing:* Metaphors & Similes — *Social Studies:* Amendments 38

Friday   *Testing:* Reading Comprehension — *Friday Fun:* Sudoku Puzzle 40

Week 4 Activities

Monday   *Math:* Mean, Median, Mode — *Writing:* Homonyms 42

Tuesday   *Reading:* Inference — *Social Studies:* Greek Mythology 44

Wednesday   *Math:* Sports Percentages — *Writing:* Persuasive Writing 46

Thursday   *Science:* System Check — *Reading:* Specialty Words 48

Friday   *Testing:* Ordering Decimals — *Friday Fun:* Complete Crossword 50

Week 5 Activities

Monday   *Math:* Excellent Exponents — *Reading:* The Escape Plan 52

Tuesday   *Science:* Food Chains — *Writing:* Review the Basics 54

Wednesday   *Math:* Square Roots — *Reading:* Popular Genres 56

Thursday   *Writing:* Hyperbole — *Social Studies:* The Preamble 58

Friday   *Testing:* Spelling Practice — *Friday Fun:* A Name Game 60

Table of Contents *(cont.)*

Week 6 Activities

Monday	*Math:* Positive & Negative — *Writing:* Connotation & Denotation	62
Tuesday	*Reading:* Symbol of Freedom — *Social Studies:* Checks & Balances	64
Wednesday	*Math:* Algebraic Equations — *Writing:* Setting the Mood	66
Thursday	*Science:* Types of Energy — *Reading:* Yes or No?	68
Friday	*Testing:* Evaluating Expressions — *Friday Fun:* Telephone Tag	70

Week 7 Activities

Monday	*Math:* Reading Graphs — *Reading:* The Fall	72
Tuesday	*Science:* Isaac Newton — *Writing:* Semicolons	74
Wednesday	*Math:* Circumference — *Reading:* Vocabulary in Context	76
Thursday	*Writing:* Go There — *Social Studies:* The First Thirteen	78
Friday	*Testing:* Synonyms — *Friday Fun:* In Other Words	80

Week 8 Activities

Monday	*Math:* Mystery Angles — *Writing:* Choose Wisely	82
Tuesday	*Reading:* News Report — *Social Studies:* The Electoral College	84
Wednesday	*Math:* Identifying Angles — *Writing:* Here's How	86
Thursday	*Science:* The Pull of Gravity — *Reading:* Bill Gates	88
Friday	*Testing:* Number Sense — *Friday Fun:* Who Lives Where?	90

Summer Reading List	92
Reading Log	95
Read and Do	96
Book Review	97
Scientific Process	98
Test-Taking Tips	99
Tough to Spell	100
Proofreading Marks	102
Measurement	103
Answer Key	104
Reward Chart	112

An Important Message

The following is an important message from the National Summer Learning Association.

Dear Parents,

Did you know that all young people experience learning losses when they don't engage in educational activities during the summer? That means some of what they've spent time learning over the preceding school year evaporates during the summer months. However, summer learning loss is something that you can help prevent. Summer is the perfect time for fun and engaging activities that can help children maintain and grow their academic skills. Here are just a few:

- Read with your child every day. Visit your local library together, and select books on subjects that interest your child.

- Ask your child's teacher for recommendations of books for summer reading. The Summer Reading List (pages 92–94 of this guide) is a good start.

- Explore parks, nature preserves, museums, and cultural centers.

- Consider every day as a day full of teachable moments. Measuring in recipes and reviewing maps before a car trip are ways to learn or reinforce a skill. Use the Learning Experiences in the back of this book for more ideas.

- Each day, set goals to accomplish. For example, do five math problems or read a chapter in a book.

- Encourage your child to complete the activities in books, such as *Summertime Learning*, to help bridge the summer learning gap.

Our vision is for every child to be safe, healthy, and engaged in learning during the summer. Learn more at *www.summerlearning.org*.

Have a *memorable* summer!

Matthew Boulay
NSLA Founder

Using This Book

As a parent, you know that summertime is a time for fun. But it can also be a time for learning and for maintaining and building upon the educational advances your child made in the previous school year. By pairing fun and learning, the books in the *Summertime Learning* series can help you keep your child on track educationally *and* allow them to have the summer break their brains and bodies need.

And to help you help your child, this resource is organized, adaptable, practical, and rewarding.

Organized

Summertime Learning: Prepare Your Child for Seventh Grade is organized around an eight-week summer vacation period. For each weekday, there are two activities. On Mondays through Thursdays, these activities include lessons in areas such as math, reading, writing, science, and social studies. Fridays offer a change of pace. Each week, the first of the Friday activities presents practice for test-taking skills. The second activity is labeled "Friday Fun," and it focuses on creativity, critical thinking, direction following, and problem solving.

Adaptable

There are many ways to use this book effectively:

- **Day by Day** — Your child can do the activities in order, beginning on the first Monday of summer vacation. For each weekday, your child will complete the two designated activities. (See the calendar on page 7.)

- **Pick and Choose** — If you do not wish to have your child work strictly in the order the activities are presented in this book, you may pick and choose any combination of pages based on your child's needs and interests.

- **All of a Kind** — If you feel that your child needs more help in one area than another, you may opt to focus on the math, reading, writing, science, or social studies activities.

In addition, the pages of this resource are perforated, which gives you the option of tearing them out if needed. If this method is chosen, a special folder or binder can be decorated and used to store the loose pages.

Extra Extra

- For a handy calendar that can set expectations and keep you and your child on schedule, see page 7 of this book.

- For Journal Topics to incorporate more writing into the weekly schedule, see page 8.

- For ways to enhance summertime reading, see pages 92–97.

- For useful reference pages in the areas of test-taking, spelling, proofreading, measurement, and more, see pages 98–103.

Practical

Parents want activity pages that take the guesswork out of how they should be used, what they are asking their child to do, and what the correct answers to the questions are. The pages in *Summertime Learning: Prepare Your Child for Seventh Grade* aim to do just that.

Several pieces of information are given in a straightforward, easy-to-read manner at the top of each activity page.

1. On one side of the activity page, the week, day, and learning area of the activity are listed. This gives parents a place to quickly check what their child is working on and to stay organized throughout the summer.

2. The opposite side features a sun icon. This is a perfect spot to place a checkmark or star to track and reward progress as your child completes the activities in the book. Using this feature will also make it easy to direct your child to the next day's activities: they can simply look for the last marked sun and work on the two pages that immediately follow.

3. The directions for each activity are written clearly and in a way that is easy to understand. Children often know how to perform an educational skill but still get questions wrong because the instructions are unclear or because they have not fully read them. You may wish to encourage your child to write a number above each line of the instructions that is asking them to do a new task.

4. Some pages include a "What To Know" box that offers a reminder of a grammar or usage rule your child will need to know in order to complete the page.

In addition, a complete answer key is included at the back of the book (pages 104–111). This can be consulted whenever any answers are in doubt.

Rewarding

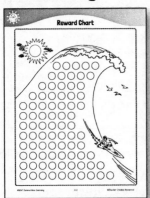

You may use the Reward Chart on page 112 of this book to keep track of the activities your child has completed. Once your child has finished a page, they can fill in a circle on the chart. In this way, the entire chart will be filled in when all 80 of the activities in this book are completed.

Weekly Calendar

If you wish, use this calendar to plan your child's work and to stay organized.

🐚 Each row of the calendar shows one week of learning. If you would find it helpful, begin by writing in the week's dates in the left-hand column.

🐚 Use the line below each learning area to make any notes that would be useful, such as the page number of the activity or the time each activity took for your child to complete.

Day	Monday	Tuesday	Wednesday	Thursday	Friday
Week 1 __/__/__ - __/__/__	☐ Math _____ ☐ Reading _____	☐ Science _____ ☐ Writing _____	☐ Math _____ ☐ Reading _____	☐ Writing _____ ☐ Social Studies _____	☐ Testing _____ ☐ Friday Fun _____
Week 2 __/__/__ - __/__/__	☐ Math _____ ☐ Writing _____	☐ Reading _____ ☐ Social Studies _____	☐ Math _____ ☐ Writing _____	☐ Science _____ ☐ Reading _____	☐ Testing _____ ☐ Friday Fun _____
Week 3 __/__/__ - __/__/__	☐ Math _____ ☐ Reading _____	☐ Science _____ ☐ Writing _____	☐ Math _____ ☐ Reading _____	☐ Writing _____ ☐ Social Studies _____	☐ Testing _____ ☐ Friday Fun _____
Week 4 __/__/__ - __/__/__	☐ Math _____ ☐ Writing _____	☐ Reading _____ ☐ Social Studies _____	☐ Math _____ ☐ Writing _____	☐ Science _____ ☐ Reading _____	☐ Testing _____ ☐ Friday Fun _____
Week 5 __/__/__ - __/__/__	☐ Math _____ ☐ Reading _____	☐ Science _____ ☐ Writing _____	☐ Math _____ ☐ Reading _____	☐ Writing _____ ☐ Social Studies _____	☐ Testing _____ ☐ Friday Fun _____
Week 6 __/__/__ - __/__/__	☐ Math _____ ☐ Writing _____	☐ Reading _____ ☐ Social Studies _____	☐ Math _____ ☐ Writing _____	☐ Science _____ ☐ Reading _____	☐ Testing _____ ☐ Friday Fun _____
Week 7 __/__/__ - __/__/__	☐ Math _____ ☐ Reading _____	☐ Science _____ ☐ Writing _____	☐ Math _____ ☐ Reading _____	☐ Writing _____ ☐ Social Studies _____	☐ Testing _____ ☐ Friday Fun _____
Week 8 __/__/__ - __/__/__	☐ Math _____ ☐ Writing _____	☐ Reading _____ ☐ Social Studies _____	☐ Math _____ ☐ Writing _____	☐ Science _____ ☐ Reading _____	☐ Testing _____ ☐ Friday Fun _____

Journal Topics

Have your child choose one of these topics once or twice per week. In a journal or notebook, have them write a few sentences in response to the chosen topic. Remind them to add enough detail so that someone else reading their responses would know the following about their topic:

🐚 who   🍦 what   🥤 when   🐚 where   ⛱ why   🦪 how

If you wish, use the following as an organizational tool. Mark the date each prompt was completed by your child.

#1 the first time I met my best friend Completed: _____	#2 an example of a modern-day hero Completed: _____	#3 the best movie I have ever seen Completed: _____
#4 the best thing a coach can do for a team Completed: _____	#5 my fondest childhood memory Completed: _____	#6 a machine I would someday like to invent Completed: _____
#7 what you would see if you looked under my bed Completed: _____	#8 what I do when I can't fall asleep Completed: _____	#9 what I would like to learn to do one day Completed: _____
#10 a talent that I have worked hard to develop Completed: _____	#11 how I would describe my favorite pair of shoes Completed: _____	#12 who I think is the greatest athlete of all time Completed: _____
#13 what I'd do if I were the richest person in the world Completed: _____	#14 the city or country I would most like to move to and live in Completed: _____	#15 the best time of day for school to start Completed: _____
#16 the most fascinating animal in the world Completed: _____	#17 the issue the world most needs to address immediately Completed: _____	#18 what I am grateful for, even on my worst days Completed: _____

Standards and Skills

Educational Standards

Each activity in *Summertime Learning: Prepare Your Child for Seventh Grade* meets one or more national educational standards. For the specific correlations of the activities to Common Core State Standards, visit *http://www.teachercreated.com/standards*.

🐚 Scroll down the alphabetical list to find the *Summertime Learning (2nd Edition)* series.

🐚 Click the link on the word **Standards** for TCR8847 Summertime Learning Grade 7 Standards.

Reinforced and Introduced Skills

The activities in *Summertime Learning: Prepare Your Child for Seventh Grade* are designed to reinforce the skills your child learned in 6th grade, as well as to introduce new skills that will be learned in 7th grade. These skills are listed below and on pages 10–11.

~~~~~~

Writing Skills

- Writes expository text

- Writes in response to personal experience

- Writes in response to literature

- Writes persuasive texts that address problems and suggest solutions

- Writes short stories and other narrative texts

- Uses strategies to draft, edit, and revise written work

- Uses paragraph form in written work

- Uses a variety of sentence structures to expand ideas

- Uses descriptive language to enhance ideas

- Uses various parts of speech — nouns, verbs, adjectives, adverbs, pronouns, prepositions, etc. — in written work

- Writes content that is appropriate to specific audiences and specific purposes

- Uses a style appropriate to specific audiences and specific purposes

- Writes in a variety of genres

- Uses the conventions of grammar in written work

- Displays an understanding of spelling, capitalization, and punctuation in written work

- Uses multiple resource materials to gather information and organizes that information

Standards and Skills (cont.)

Reinforced and Introduced Skills (cont.)

Reading Skills

- Understands and adjusts purposes for reading
- Understands grade-appropriate reading vocabulary
- Uses strategies to enhance reading vocabulary
- Reads a variety of literary passages and text
- Reads a variety of literary genres
- Knows the defining features of various literary genres
- Understands elements of plot and character development
- Understands the use of specific literary devices
- Understands how language can be used to convey mood and meaning
- Understands purposes and uses of point of view
- Makes connections between characters and plot developments in a text and those in their own life
- Summarizes and paraphrases information in texts
- Uses new information to adjust and expand personal understanding
- Draws conclusions and makes inferences based on both explicit and implicit information

Mathematics Skills

- Uses a variety of strategies to solve problems
- Understands that different problem-solving methods have advantages and disadvantages
- Determines the information required to solve a problem and chooses methods for obtaining that information
- Understands that written symbols represent mathematical ideas
- Adds, subtracts, multiplies, and divides integers and other rational numbers
- Understands the correct order of operations for solving math computations
- Understands the role of positive and negative integers in the number system
- Understands the properties of operations with rational numbers

Standards and Skills (cont.)

Reinforced and Introduced Skills (cont.)

Mathematics Skills (cont.)

- Understands how math can be used to solve real-world problems
- Adds and subtracts fractions with unlike denominators; multiplies and divides fractions
- Understands the characteristics and uses of exponents and scientific notation
- Understands the concepts of ratios, proportions, and percentages
- Understands how formulas can be used to find measures
- Solves problems involving perimeters or areas of various shapes
- Understands that linear measurements are recorded in units
- Understands that area measurements are recorded in square units
- Understands that volume measurements are recorded in cubic units
- Understands the defining properties of two- and three-dimensional figures
- Understands how to read the data represented in various charts, tables, and graphs
- Understands how to apply data to create various charts, tables, and graphs
- Understands how to determine probability
- Understands when to use estimation
- Understands how to find averages when given a set of numbers
- Understands how predictions can be based on data and probabilities
- Understands basic operations on algebraic operations
- Understands the concepts of similarity and congruency
- Understands the use of variables to solve math problems

Products & Quotients

Directions: Solve each problem. Show your work.

1.	2.	3.	4.
$\begin{array}{r} 4{,}411 \\ \times\ \ \ 13 \\ \hline \end{array}$	$\begin{array}{r} 8{,}476 \\ \times\ \ \ 34 \\ \hline \end{array}$	$\begin{array}{r} 32{,}566 \\ \times\ \ \ 145 \\ \hline \end{array}$	$\begin{array}{r} 4{,}373 \\ \times\ \ \ 810 \\ \hline \end{array}$

5.	6.	7.	8.
$\begin{array}{r} 36{,}592 \\ \times\ \ \ 484 \\ \hline \end{array}$	$\begin{array}{r} 65{,}349 \\ \times\ \ \ 785 \\ \hline \end{array}$	$\begin{array}{r} 175{,}797 \\ \times\ \ \ 153 \\ \hline \end{array}$	$\begin{array}{r} 567{,}899 \\ \times\ \ \ 346 \\ \hline \end{array}$

9.	10.	11.	12.
$24\overline{)67{,}296}$	$31\overline{)59{,}737}$	$27\overline{)33{,}021}$	$123\overline{)79{,}089}$

13.	14.	15.	16.
$910\overline{)29{,}120}$	$153\overline{)213{,}588}$	$619\overline{)341{,}688}$	$11\overline{)1{,}364{,}000}$

Nine Brains, No Bones

Directions: Read the nonfiction passage in the box. To answer the questions below, circle the letter beside each correct response.

Imagine a creature that has one beak, three hearts, eight arms, nine brains, no bones, blue blood, flesh-softening venom, and a sac of black ink. What kind of alien monster could this creature be?

Actually, what is being described is no monster at all. It is an octopus, and it poses very little danger to humans. (The Australian blue-ringed octopus is the only variety whose venom is strong enough to kill a person.) All of these strange adaptations allow the octopus to survive and **thrive** in its natural habitat.

For feeding, the octopus uses its strong beak to bite prey and crack open clam shells. It uses its venom to soften the flesh of its prey, making that flesh easier to suck out of a shell.

For defense, the octopus is able to squeeze into small cracks in rocks and hide. Having no bones makes that possible. The octopus can also release a cloud of black ink to confuse predators.

The animal's three hearts pump blood through its gills. The copper in this blood makes it blue and helps the octopus use oxygen better in the cold waters it calls home. In addition to a brain in its head, the octopus also has a tiny brain in each of its eight arms. This intelligent animal can use tools and remember the problems it has previously solved.

1. Which answer best states why an octopus would squirt black ink into the water?

   A. The octopus is trying to show dominance.

   B. The octopus is trying to escape from a predator.

   C. The octopus is trying to soften the flesh of its prey.

   D. The octopus is trying to show how intelligent it is.

2. What is a synonym for the word *thrive* in the second paragraph of the passage?

   A. adapt   C. ingest

   B. strive   D. succeed

3. Which word best seems to describe the author's feelings about octopuses?

   A. frightened   C. amazed

   B. envious   D. disgusted

4. Which of these features would alert you that an octopus could be dangerous to you?

   A. black ink   C. blue blood

   B. copper blood   D. blue rings

Earth's Layers

Directions: Use the words in the Word Bank and the labeled diagram of Earth's layers to complete the chart below. Write a description of each layer.

Word Bank   core   mantle   lithosphere   hydrosphere   atmosphere

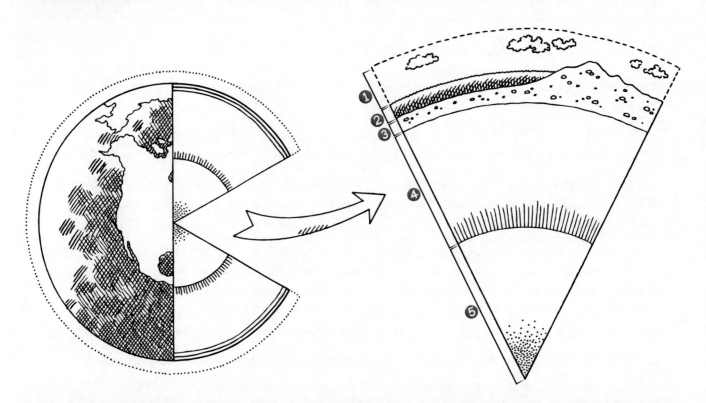

Label	Layer Name	Description
1		
2		
3		
4		
5		

Run-On Sentences

What to Know

In the first type of run-on sentence, the sentence is missing punctuation and/or a coordinating conjunction.

Examples: She went to Australia she saw a kangaroo. (run-on)
She went to Australia. She saw a kangaroo. (correct)
She went to Australia, and she saw a kangaroo. (correct)

Directions: Study the run-on sentences below. Fix them by adding a period or a comma and a coordinating conjunction. Choose from *and, but,* or *so.*

1. Molly bought groceries she also bought flowers.

2. Tracy swims every day she also jogs three miles.

3. Hawaii is a state now it was not one until 1959.

4. Tomorrow is a national holiday schools and banks will be closed.

5. The singer's voice was tired she didn't cancel the concert.

6. We visited St. Louis we did not go inside the Gateway Arch.

7. My dog loves the forest he runs all over, sniffing trees.

8. The girl painted a picture she hoped to give it to her mother.

What to Know

In the second type of run-on sentence, the sentence is missing a conjunction.

Examples: We love the baseball team, we see a game every Saturday. (run-on)
We love the baseball team, and we see a game every Saturday. (correct)
We love the baseball team, so we see a game every Saturday. (correct)

Directions: Study the run-on sentences below. Fix them by adding a conjunction.

9. She loves hot chocolate, she drinks three cups a day.

10. The soccer team won the match, they earned a trophy

11. A bird made a nest in Mark's chimney, he had to call a chimney sweep.

12. Grandpa taught me to fish, we caught three trout.

13. Honeybees have a hive in that tree, don't get stung.

14. She trained hard for four years, her hard work paid off.

15. The photographer took many photos, we never saw them.

Time and Distance

Directions: The community park is sponsoring a ride-a-thon. People can bring their bicycles, skateboards, scooters, or skates. Help compute time and distance for the riders. Use a separate piece of paper to show your work.

What to Know

📖 Time is computed by dividing the distance traveled by the rate of speed. $t = \frac{d}{r}$

📖 Distance is computed by multiplying the rate of speed times the amount of time expended. $d = rt$

1. Kyle rode his skateboard for 40 minutes at an average speed of 80 feet per minute.

   What distance did he travel? _____ feet

2. Ashley rode her skateboard 3,200 feet at 80 feet per minute.

   How many minutes did she ride? _____ minutes

3. Olive rode her bicycle for 50 minutes at an average speed of 200 feet per minute.

   How many feet did she travel? _____ feet

4. Jeffrey rode his in-line skates for 99 minutes at an average speed of 72 feet per minute.

   What distance did Jeffrey travel? _____ feet

5. Veronica rode her motorized scooter 31,680 feet at an average speed of 80 feet per minute.

   How many minutes did she ride her scooter? _____ minutes

6. Gavin rode his scooter at 86 feet per minute for 90 minutes.

   How many feet did he ride? _____ feet

7. Marie rode her mountain bike for 240 minutes at an average speed of 100 feet per minute.

   How far did she ride? _____ feet

8. Louise rode her scooter 40,240 feet at 80 feet per minute.

   How many minutes did she ride her scooter? _____ minutes

9. Jonathan skated 32,800 feet at 80 feet per minute.

   How many minutes did he skate? _____ minutes

10. Kristin rode her bicycle for 320 minutes at 95 feet per minute.

    How many feet did she ride? _____ feet

Fact or Opinion?

What to Know	A *fact* is true and can be proven. An *opinion* is someone's thoughts or feelings about an issue.

Examples: *Fact*—Dinosaurs roamed the planet many years ago.
Opinion—Dinosaurs were the scariest creatures that ever roamed the planet.

Directions: For each statement, write **fact** if it is a fact. Write **opinion** if it is an opinion.

_____ 1. There are twelve months in a year.

_____ 2. Chocolate is the best flavor of ice cream.

_____ 3. The best night to watch television is Friday.

_____ 4. Five feet is equal to 60 inches.

_____ 5. There are an infinite number of numbers.

_____ 6. Everyone should say "please" and "thank you."

_____ 7. Social studies is the best subject.

_____ 8. Running a mile is harder than swimming a mile.

_____ 9. Dogs make better pets than cats.

_____ 10. Nine plus seven equals 16.

_____ 11. Breakfast is the best meal of the day.

_____ 12. George Washington was the first president of the United States.

_____ 13. Europe is a continent.

_____ 14. The Atlantic Ocean is much nicer than the Pacific Ocean.

_____ 15. The Atlantic Ocean is much smaller than the Pacific Ocean.

Sensory Words

What to Know	Sensory words are words that describe how something feels, how something looks, how something sounds, how something smells, or how something tastes.

Example: The tang of the rhubarb made my tongue tingle. [*taste* (tang) and *feel* (tingle)]

Directions: Write a sentence that uses two of the five senses to describe each of the following.

1. pizza _____

_____

2. trash truck _____

_____

3. snake _____

_____

4. tennis shoes _____

_____

5. desert _____

_____

6. dessert _____

_____

7. surprise _____

_____

8. music concert _____

_____

Where in the World?

Directions: List the countries in the Country Box under the appropriate continents.

Country Box

Switzerland	Kenya	Costa Rica	Canada	Saudi Arabia
Libya	United Kingdom	Brazil	Venezuela	Iran
Japan	Spain	Israel	France	Nicaragua
Ethiopia	Vietnam	Poland	Chile	Nigeria
El Salvador	Ecuador	Thailand	Cuba	Morocco
Iraq	United States	Sweden	Algeria	Egypt
China	Germany	Uruguay	Philippines	Guatemala
Italy	India	Bolivia	Angola	Greece
Mexico	Sudan	Colombia	Peru	Panama
Paraguay	Ireland	Tanzania	Hungary	Argentina

Africa

Asia

Europe

North America

South America

Complete Sentences

Directions: Read each group of words carefully. Find either the complete sentence or the fragment. Fill in the correct answer circle.

Sample

Find the fragment.

Ⓐ **And bought popcorn too.**

Ⓒ The film was so scary I screamed!

Ⓑ I went to the movies.

Ⓓ I took my little sister to the movies.

---

1. Find the fragment.

Ⓐ I sing in the choir at church.

Ⓑ Late for my choir practice.

Ⓒ We rehearse two nights a week.

Ⓓ My mother sings in the choir, too.

5. Find the sentence.

Ⓐ Was big and gray.

Ⓑ The trunk and the legs.

Ⓒ The elephant weighed over a ton.

Ⓓ An unbelievable amount of food.

---

2. Find the sentence.

Ⓔ So fast I nearly tripped over my feet!

Ⓕ And an entire flight of stairs.

Ⓖ I overslept and almost missed the bus.

Ⓗ Slowed down so I could get on.

6. Find the sentence.

Ⓔ They lost by thirteen points.

Ⓕ Fumbled the ball twice.

Ⓖ Was injured in the third quarter.

Ⓗ The quarterback and the kicker.

---

3. Find the fragment.

Ⓐ The costume was very uncomfortable.

Ⓑ The trousers were way too big.

Ⓒ I had to shorten the trousers by about three inches.

Ⓓ Feathers and sequins on the sleeves.

7. Find the fragment.

Ⓐ The characters were so lifelike.

Ⓑ My favorite book by.

Ⓒ It has a surprise ending.

Ⓓ The author is from Alaska.

---

4. Find the fragment.

Ⓔ It rained for nearly twelve hours.

Ⓕ Flooded and filled with debris.

Ⓖ I saw a car floating in the street.

Ⓗ The playground was destroyed.

8. Find the sentence.

Ⓔ Made hot dogs and baked beans.

Ⓕ The picnic was really.

Ⓖ Most of the food.

Ⓗ There was a lot of food at the picnic.

Magic Math

Directions: Follow the instructions below to work out an astonishing math riddle. Complete the tasks in the order they are given. For each one, write the equation in the third column and the answer in the fourth column. If needed, use scratch paper to work some of the equations.

Step	Task	Equation	Answer
1	Write the number of the month in which you were born. (For example, if you were born in June, write **6**.) Multiply your answer to by **4**.		
2	Add **13** to your answer from #1.		
3	Multiply your answer to #2 by **25**.		
4	Subtract **200** from your answer to #3.		
5	Take your answer to #4 and add to it the day of the month on which you were born. (For example, if you were born on June 9, add **9**.)		
6	Multiply your answer to #5 by **2**.		
7	Subtract **40** from your answer to #6.		
8	Multiply your answer to #7 by **50**.		
9	Take your answer to #8 and add to it the last two digits of the year of your birth.		
10	Subtract **10,500** from your answer to #9.		

Look closely at your last answer. Explain the significance of this number.

_____

_____

Liquid Measurement

Directions: Use the boxed information to help you convert the listed measurements and answer the questions.

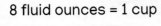

Liquid Measurement

8 fluid ounces = 1 cup

2 cups = 1 pint

2 pints = 1 quart

4 quarts = 1 gallon

Part 1

1. 2 cups = _____ fluid ounces

2. 8 quarts = _____ gallons

3. 1 gallon = _____ fluid ounces

4. 1 quart = _____ cups

5. 3 quarts = _____ pints

6. 24 fluid ounces = _____ cups

7. 2 gallons = _____ pints

8. 4 cups = _____ pints

Part 2

9. How many cups are in 3 quarts? _____

10. How many fluid ounces are in 4 pints? _____

11. How many quarts are in 5 gallons? _____

12. How many cups are in 9 pints? _____

13. How many pints are in 3 gallons? _____

14. How many gallons are in 64 cups? _____

Part 3

15. Why is it important to know how to convert measurements? List two reasons.

    Reason #1: _____

    _____

    Reason #2: _____

    _____

Phrases & Clauses

Sometimes a writer adds information to a sentence to make it more interesting. This information is in the form of a nonessential phrase or clause. A nonessential phrase or clause adds information that the reader doesn't need in order to understand the basic meaning of the sentence. Therefore, it could be left out without changing the main idea of the sentence. Use commas to set off a nonessential phrase or clause.

Nonessential Phrases and Clauses Need Commas

The sunset, *glowing in the evening dusk*, looked like a ball of fire.

(The sunset looked like a ball of fire.)

Andy Warhol, *who was a famous artist from the 1970s*, created portraits using a silk-screening technique.

(Andy Warhol created portraits using a silk-screening technique.)

Do not set off an essential phrase or clause with commas. An essential phrase or clause cannot be omitted without changing the main idea of the sentence.

Essential Phrases and Clauses Do Not Need Commas

All students *who witnessed the incident* must report to the principal's office immediately.

(All students must report to the principal's office immediately. *Which students?*)

The horror movie *that you recommended to me* is not available for online streaming.

(The horror movie is not available for online streaming. *Which horror movie?*)

Directions: Read each sentence. Draw a line under the phrase or clause contained within the sentence. If the phrase or clause is nonessential, set it off with commas.

1. All farmers who are growing the new hybrid of wheat are expected to have a good harvest.

2. Kareem Abdul-Jabbar who holds several NBA records retired from basketball in 1989.

3. Founded in 1636 Harvard College is the oldest college in the United States.

4. The inventions created by Thomas Edison have changed the way people live around the world.

5. Jose has a tremendous fear of spiders which is known as arachnophobia.

6. The championship cup dusty and filled with coins sat on the highest shelf.

Story Sequence

Directions: Read the following story, then number the events in the order in which they happened.

This is Aaron's third year in medical school. He began medical school at University School of Medicine after he graduated from Mount Vernon College. Now he is both working in a lab and taking classes.

When Aaron was in the eighth grade, he visited a doctor on Career Day and learned that being a doctor was a great way to help people. Aaron decided that he wanted to be a doctor someday. He pursued his dream by going to college.

At Mount Vernon College, Aaron took a lot of chemistry and biology classes. Some of these classes were review, though, because Aaron had also taken chemistry and biology courses in high school. Also, while in high school, Aaron volunteered at the hospital, and these experiences helped him in college as well. Aaron worked very hard through college and earned good grades.

Although he is in his third year of medical school, Aaron has not yet decided what type of doctor he would like to be. Aaron enjoys research and may decide to use his medical degree to do research or teach. Aaron is glad that he decided to attend medical school.

_____ Aaron graduated from Mount Vernon College.

_____ Aaron took a lot of chemistry and biology classes at Mount Vernon College.

_____ Aaron volunteered at the hospital.

_____ Aaron is in his third year of medical school.

_____ Aaron decided in the eighth grade that he wanted to be a doctor.

_____ Aaron began medical school at University School of Medicine.

_____ Aaron pursued his dream by going to college.

Mummies

Directions: Use the information in the passage to complete the statements below.

Ancient Egyptians believed that after a person died, that person went on to live in the afterlife. They believed that a person would need their body in this afterlife. For this reason the ancient Egyptians developed the practice of mummification, which prevented a body from decaying as fast as it normally would after death.

The process of turning a body into a mummy took about 70 days. It was performed by priests called *embalmers*. They were specially trained in the mummification process.

The first thing the ancient Egyptians did was remove all of the moisture from the body. This was called *dehydration*. Next, they would remove all of the internal organs. They used a long wire and pulled the brain out through the nose. A small incision, or cut, was made in the side of the body through which the liver, lungs, and other parts were removed.

These internal organs were washed in oil and then put in canopic jars. The lids of the canopic jars were carved with the heads of special gods who protected the organs. The heart was left in the body. The ancient Egyptians believed that the heart was the organ of life force and intellect and that the person would need it in the afterlife.

After the organs were removed, the body was covered in a kind of salt called *natron*. This salt drew even more moisture from the body. After about 35 days, the body would be wrapped in linens. The arms, legs, and even fingers were wrapped individually. The embalmers put amulets or charms inside of the linens to protect the person in the afterlife. A death mask was placed onto the mummy. Then the mummy was put in a coffin.

Archaeologists have found several Egyptian mummies, including Tutankhamun, Ramesses I and II, and Seti I. Ancient Egyptian mummies have been x-rayed and scanned with modern equipment. This helps scientists learn valuable things about the ancient Egyptians, including what they ate and diseases that they suffered from.

1. Ancient Eygptians mummified their dead because _____

   _____.

2. It took about _____ days to mummify a body.

3. After they were removed from the body, internal organs were stored in _____

   _____.

4. Priests who performed mummifications were called _____.

5. By studying mummies, scientists have learned _____

   _____.

Fraction Frenzy

Directions: Solve these fraction problems. Be sure to watch the operation signs and to reduce your answers to simplest form. Circle your final answers.

1. $\frac{1}{10} + \frac{4}{12} =$	9. $9\frac{10}{12} - 5\frac{6}{7} =$
2. $\frac{3}{5} - \frac{3}{12} =$	10. $8\frac{5}{6} - 1\frac{4}{5} =$
3. $3\frac{3}{6} - 2\frac{3}{4} =$	11. $10\frac{3}{7} + 2\frac{6}{10} =$
4. $8\frac{4}{7} + 3\frac{2}{10} =$	12. $1\frac{6}{8} + 3\frac{2}{6} =$
5. $2\frac{2}{3} \times \frac{1}{2} =$	13. $\frac{1}{9} \div \frac{9}{16} =$
6. $4\frac{2}{7} \times 2\frac{1}{8} =$	14. $12\frac{1}{8} \times \frac{2}{3} =$
7. $\frac{4}{8} \div \frac{9}{16} =$	15. $\frac{1}{6} \times 3\frac{8}{9} =$
8. $\frac{3}{9} \div \frac{12}{22} =$	16. $\frac{8}{10} \div \frac{3}{6} =$

Can You Elaborate?

Directions: Elaborate the simple sentences below by answering at least two of the following: who, what, what kind, where, when, why, and how. Rewrite the complete sentence. The first one has been done for you.

1. The students studied history. <u>The 8th grade students at Hill Middle School studied United States history last summer.</u>

2. They went to the theater. _____

3. The zoo is fun. _____

4. The student was mad. _____

5. The boy likes animals. _____

6. The woman gave the orders. _____

7. The kids crossed the street. _____

8. The contestants swam in the competition. _____

9. The cards were arranged in order. _____

10. The bookstore specializes in novels. _____

More Than Planets

There is so much more in the universe than the planets and their moons. Comets, asteroids, and meteoroids all have their places in the solar system.

A comet is made of ice, rock, and dust from space. When a comet goes near the sun, the sun's heat melts the ice. The comet then gives off gas and dust, making it appear as if the comet has a tail. Comets orbit the sun, just as the planets do; however, the orbit of a comet is not as elliptical as the orbit of the planets.

Other astronomical bodies that orbit in space are asteroids. Asteroids are rocky bodies that vary in shape. An area between Mars and Jupiter is known as an asteroid belt. This is where the majority of asteroids orbit in the solar system.

Meteoroids are also part of the solar system. Like asteroids, they have a rocky shape; however, meteoroids are smaller than asteroids. Many scientists believe meteoroids are just small pieces of asteroids. When a meteoroid enters Earth's atmosphere, it starts to burn and give off energy. As it burns, it leaves a streak of light in the night sky. This light is then called a meteor. Some people refer to these bright streaks of light as shooting stars. If part of the meteor survives and lands on Earth, it is called a meteorite.

Directions: Use the information in the passage above to help answer the questions.

1. A large number of asteroids, clustered together form an _____ between Mars and Jupiter.

2. Small bodies, such as asteroids and meteoroids, are part of the _____, just as the planets and their moons are.

3. When the heat from the sun melts the ice in a comet, the comet forms a _____ that can be seen from Earth.

4. _____ have rocky shapes that are smaller than asteroids.

5. Scientists believe that a meteoroid was probably once part of an _____.

6. A meteor that survives and lands on Earth becomes a _____.

7. As a meteoroid burns up and gives off energy, a bright streak of light forms; this light is

   called a _____.

8. Why do you think it is important for people to study the smaller bodies in our solar system?

   _____

   _____

Big Foot Vocabulary

Directions: Find the meaning of each underlined word in the paragraph below. Put the letter of the answer on the blank line. Use the definitions in the box below to help you.

A. evil	C. careless	E. a member of a habitat
B. to roam all around	D. a form of transportation	F. to cleverly avoid

1. _____ People say that Big Foot ¹rambles through the woods. He has very big feet, and

2. _____ he uses them. No other ²conveyance is necessary! People have seen his shadow in

   Oregon. Others have reported seeing him in Canada. People believe that Big Foot

3. _____ is a beast, but not ³malevolent. Although nobody has been harmed by Big Foot, it

4. _____ would still be ⁴feckless to approach him. The best policy seems to be "Keep your

5. _____ distance." So far, Big Foot has always been able to ⁵elude those who search for

6. _____ him. He is a ⁶denizen of thick, dark forests, and the woods provide his cover.

Directions: Fill in the blanks with your new words.

7. "Escape" is similar to _____.

8. A cart or a carriage is a _____.

9. A violent character is very _____.

10. Someone who walks around is like someone who _____.

11. "Reckless" has a similar meaning as _____.

12. A creature of a place is a _____.

Directions: Use each new word in a sentence.

13. _____

14. _____

15. _____

16. _____

17. _____

18. _____

Multiply & Divide Fractions

Directions: Read each problem. Fill in the circle that shows the correct answer in its lowest terms.

Sample

A. $2\frac{3}{5} \times 1\frac{7}{8} =$

Ⓐ $\frac{8}{40}$ Ⓒ $\frac{1}{5}$

Ⓑ $18\frac{1}{5}$ Ⓓ $4\frac{7}{8}$ ●

B. $\frac{3}{9} \div 1\frac{2}{10} =$

Ⓔ $\frac{5}{18}$ ●   Ⓖ $\frac{6}{90}$

Ⓕ $\frac{2}{3}$ Ⓗ $4\frac{3}{2}$

---

1. $2\frac{4}{5} \times \frac{2}{3} =$

Ⓐ $\frac{13}{15}$ Ⓒ $1\frac{13}{15}$

Ⓑ $\frac{15}{13}$ Ⓓ none of these

2. $\frac{9}{10} \div 7 =$

Ⓔ $\frac{9}{70}$ Ⓖ $\frac{63}{70}$

Ⓕ $\frac{70}{9}$ Ⓗ $\frac{70}{62}$

3. $2\frac{1}{5} \times 7\frac{9}{12} =$

Ⓐ $\frac{1}{20}$ Ⓒ $\frac{3}{60}$

Ⓑ $17\frac{3}{60}$ Ⓓ $17\frac{1}{20}$

4. $2\frac{4}{5} \times 1\frac{7}{8} =$

Ⓔ $\frac{490}{540}$ Ⓖ $\frac{10}{12}$

Ⓕ $\frac{90}{108}$ Ⓗ $5\frac{1}{4}$

5. $3 \times \frac{7}{9} =$

Ⓐ $2\frac{1}{3}$ Ⓒ $\frac{140}{83}$

Ⓑ $2\frac{3}{9}$ Ⓓ none of these

6. $4\frac{3}{20} \div 7 =$

Ⓔ $\frac{581}{20}$ Ⓖ $\frac{140}{83}$

Ⓕ $\frac{83}{140}$ Ⓗ none of these

7. $10\frac{2}{9} \times 7\frac{1}{8} =$

Ⓐ $72\frac{30}{36}$ Ⓒ 72

Ⓑ $72\frac{5}{6}$ Ⓓ none of these

8. $\frac{2}{3} \div 3\frac{1}{3} =$

Ⓔ $\frac{1}{6}$ Ⓖ $\frac{4}{9}$

Ⓕ $\frac{5}{1}$ Ⓗ $\frac{1}{5}$

Rhyming Riddles

Directions: These riddles can be answered with two rhyming words. The first one has been done for you. Use the initials in parentheses to help you guess the rest.

1. an overweight feline (f.c.)

   fat cat

2. a thief in a library (b.c.)

   _____

3. a purple gorilla (g.a.)

   _____

4. a 10 cent fruit (d.l.)

   _____

5. an ideal home for a bird (b.n.)

   _____

6. a man's odd facial hair (w.b.)

   _____

7. a fast moving baby bird (q.c.)

   _____

8. a friendly potato (s.b.)

   _____

9. loud noises made by a coat (j.r.)

   _____

10. a less narrow arachnid (w.s.)

    _____

11. a lollipop lying on the beach (s.c.)

    _____

12. a thing to stop a cobra's progress (s.b.)

    _____

Decimals Crossword

Directions: Solve the problems below, then write the answers in the number puzzle. Be sure to include the decimal points in the puzzle. See #1 Across. It has been done for you.

— **Across** —

1. .217 ÷ .7 = ___.31___

3. 3.90 ÷ .03 = _____

4. .72 ÷ .03 = _____

5. 3.12 ÷ .08 = _____

6. 9.16 ÷ .08 = _____

9. .570 ÷ .08 = _____

11. .552 ÷ .03 = _____

12. .153 ÷ .03 = _____

13. 9.80 ÷ .05 = _____

14. 3.08 ÷ .7 = _____

15. .488 ÷ .08 = _____

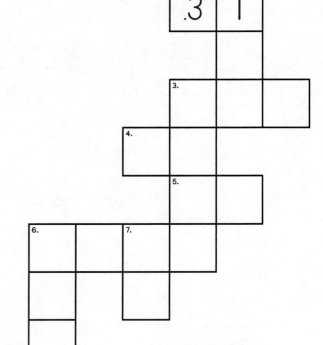

— **Down** —

2. 4.1 × .3 = _____

3. 41 × 3.5 = _____

6. 2.5 × 6.1 = _____

7. 1.1 × 4 = _____

8. 9 × .9 = _____

9. .5 × 14.95 = _____

10. 4.3 × .5 = _____

11. .2 × 5.8 = _____

13. .04 × 36.5 = _____

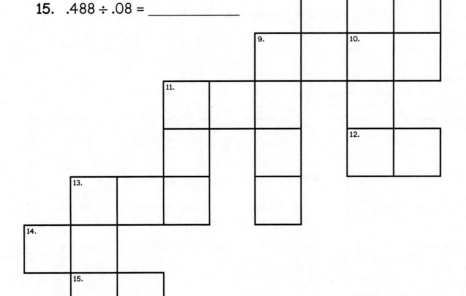

Nelson Mandela

Directions: Read the nonfiction passage below and answer the questions that follow.

Nelson Mandela was born in Transkei, South Africa, on July 18, 1918. He was the first member of his family to attend school. A Methodist teacher gave him the name "Nelson" at school. He continued in school and later attended the University of South Africa in Johannesburg. He became a lawyer representing those who would otherwise go without legal assistance.

Mandela was first involved in nonviolent protests but was eventually arrested for **treason** and placed in prison. He was fighting against apartheid and the treatment of his people. Apartheid was the practice of keeping the races separated in South Africa. Locked in his cell for years on end, Nelson's spirit was not broken. Nelson Mandela spent 27 years in prison. Most of this time was spent in a tiny cell on Robben Island. His captivity became widely publicized. He was considered a terrorist when he was imprisoned, but as time wore on, it became apparent that he was treated unjustly in his fight to end apartheid.

Once released from prison, Nelson Mandela went on to receive hundreds of awards. He received the Nobel Peace Prize, which many felt was also a tribute to the people of South Africa as much as to him. On April 27, 1994, Nelson Mandela was elected President of South Africa. He served until 1999. He continued to push for peace throughout the world. In South Africa, he is known as *Madiba*, which is an honorary title. Nelson Mandela continues to inspire many, even long after his death in 2013.

1. What can you infer about why Nelson was so successful in life?

    A. People felt sorry for him and took pity on him.

    B. He eventually got the vision of his life.

    C. He learned great lessons and was able to overcome obstacles and work hard.

    D. He was able to become president.

2. What is the meaning of the word *treason* as used in the second paragraph?

    A. disloyalty

    B. selfishness

    C. violence

    D. protest

3. Which of the following statements can be identified as true after reading the passage?

    A. Nelson Mandela spent his life seeking restitution for his treatment.

    B. Nelson Mandela was a perfect person.

    C. Nelson Mandela went on to inspire millions because of his experiences.

    D. Apartheid no longer exists on the African continent.

Inherited Traits

Directions: Read the information below about genetic traits and Punnett squares. Then, answer the questions about the blood–type Punnett square and complete the Punnett square for freckles.

Offspring receive half of their chromosomes from the female parent and half from the male parent. Therefore, they inherit traits from both parents. Traits can either be dominant or recessive. If a trait is dominant, it means that it is seen in the offspring. If a trait is recessive, it may not be seen in the offspring. For a recessive trait to be seen in offspring, the offspring must receive a recessive gene from both parents.

A Punnett square is a diagram that illustrates all of the possible genetic combinations that can occur with a given set of parents. A dominant trait is represented with a capital letter and a recessive trait is represented with a lowercase letter.

The Punnett square to the right shows the possible blood type outcomes for a child of parents with Type A and Type O blood. Type A is the dominant trait (A), and Type O is recessive (o).

	o	o
A	Ao	Ao
o	oo	oo

1. If the child receives Ao, it will have Type _____ blood.

2. If the child receives oo, it will have Type _____ blood.

3. What are the chances that the child will have Type A blood? _____

4. Complete this Punnett square for freckles.

Parent 1

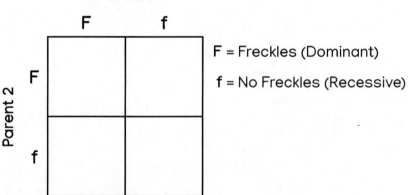

F = Freckles (Dominant)

f = No Freckles (Recessive)

5. What are the chances this child will not have freckles? _____

Quotation Marks

> **What to Know**
>
> **Quotation marks** should be used anytime someone speaks. One set of quotation marks should be placed at the beginning of the quote and one set at the end.

Examples: "Where did you come from?" she asked the ghost.
Peter made a cake, then shouted, "Happy Birthday!" to his father.

Directions: Study the sentences below. Add quotation marks where needed.

1. Are you going to take the trash out? Mom asked David.

2. David yawned. I'm busy playing video games, he said.

3. It won't take itself out, Mom reminded him.

4. I'll do it! David exclaimed.

5. He'll forget until tonight, Mom muttered to the dog.

6. Woof! barked the dog, sniffing the trash can.

7. David! yelled Mom. Take out this trash now!

8. Okay, okay, said David. I'm turning off the game.

9. He took out the trash. It stinks, he said.

10. I'm finished, he told Mother. Can I have my allowance?

Directions: Now, write down a conversation between Jay and Mari, who are discussing the big skateboarding competition scheduled for this Saturday. Use at least 6 sentences. Don't forget the quotation marks.

_____

_____

_____

_____

_____

_____

_____

Interest in Banking

The People's Bank
(Interest Earned Per Month)

$25–$250	No Interest		$751–$1,000	2%
$251–$500	1%		$1,001–$10,000	3%
$501–$750	1.5%		More than $10,000	3.5%

Directions: Use the chart to find the interest earned on each savings account.

Jamie opens a savings account with $1,500.00. She leaves the money in the account for 1 month.

1. How much interest does she earn? _____

2. What is her ending balance? _____

Lee opens a savings account with $250.00. Lee leaves the money in the account for 2 months.

3. How much interest does Lee earn the first month? _____

4. How much interest does Lee earn the second month? _____

5. Explain answers 3 and 4. _____

_____

Suppose Lee adds $100 to the account at the beginning of the second month.

6. How much interest would Lee earn that month? _____

7. How much money would Lee have in the account at the end of that month? _____

Curtis opens a savings account with $9,800.00. He leaves the money in the bank for 1 month.

8. How much interest does he earn? _____

9. What would his balance be after earning that interest? _____

10. With this new balance in his account, how much
    interest would he earn the next month? _____

Vocabulary Practice

Directions: Choose from the verbs and adjectives in the box to find the best word to complete each sentence below. You may need to form plurals or add other endings to some words. Use each word only once.

Verbs		Adjectives	
compose	overwhelm	grueling	priceless
conform	personalize	infuriating	random
contribute	recede	permanent	simultaneous

1. Beethoven _____ some of his greatest music after he had lost most of his hearing.

2. The ink left a _____ stain that no amount of cleaning could remove from his favorite coat.

3. For an extra $5, I had my backpack _____ with my initials.

4. They waited for the waves to _____ before attempting to cross the cove's narrow shoreline.

5. After a _____ 20-mile hike, the group finally reached its destination.

6. Video showed that the two finishes were _____, and the race was declared a tie.

7. Rae _____ 3 hours of her time every Saturday to help clean up County Park.

8. After a recent incident, a guard is now stationed near the _____ artwork at all times.

9. Coach Frank found it _____ when the referee made the wrong call, costing his team a win.

10. The increased demand for the popular toy _____ many stores and led to long lines and poor service.

11. If you are going to be a member of a team, then you must _____ to its rules.

12. I know it's supposed to be _____, but why does it seem like my name never gets picked out of the hat?

Metaphors & Similes

What to Know

A **metaphor** is one kind of comparison. A metaphor is a direct comparison that implies that a thing may be thought of as something else.

Example: The new bed is a fluffy cloud.

Part 1 Directions: Rewrite each description. Use a metaphor to make a comparison.

1. The smell of the pumpkin pie hit me as I walked in.

   _____

2. The sunset color spread across the sky.

   _____

3. The fireworks went splashing into the dark night.

   _____

4. The baby's cry woke everyone in the house.

   _____

5. The careless boy knocked over many things in the antique store.

   _____

What to Know

A **simile** is a type of metaphor that uses words such as *like* or *as* to make comparisons between things.

Example: The new bed was as comfortable as a fluffy cloud.

Part 2 Directions: Write a sentence that includes a simile and compares the following things to other things.

1. rain _____

2. chair _____

3. scream _____

4. cereal _____

5. math test _____

6. game _____

7. dessert _____

8. desert _____

Amendments

On September 17, 1787, the Constitution of the United States was read in Philadelphia, Pennsylvania. It took two years for all 13 states to approve this plan for governing their new nation. The first 10 amendments, ratified on June 8, 1789, are called the Bill of Rights. While the Constitution established the power of the government, the Bill of Rights asserted the rights of individual citizens. Since then, additional amendments to the Constitution have been added as needed. Some of them are described in the activity below.

Directions: For each question, write the number of each amendment described. Then, add or subtract the numbers as indicated to find the final answer. A book about the U.S. Constitution or an online source may be needed for this activity. The first answer has been given.

1. repealed prohibition ___21___ + limited president to two terms ___22___ = ___43___

2. sum from #1 _____ + gave women the right to vote _____ = _____

3. sum from #2 _____ – how to replace a president unable to serve _____ = _____

4. difference from #3 _____ + outlawed the poll tax _____ = _____

5. sum from #4 _____ – gave Washington D.C. residents the right to vote for president _____ = _____

6. difference from #5 _____ + outlawed the drinking of alcohol _____ = _____

7. sum from #6 _____ + change inauguration date to January 20 _____ = _____

8. sum from #7 _____ – lowered the voting age to 18 _____ = _____

Check Your Math!

Your answer should equal the total number of U.S. states once Hawaii became a state in 1959.

Reading Comprehension

Directions: Read the passage carefully. Then, answer the questions that follow. Fill in the correct answer circle.

The Loch Ness Monster

Ever heard of Nessie? There is a legend that says that Nessie is a giant sea monster that lives in Loch Ness in the country of Scotland. A loch is a kind of lake, and for many years there have been reports of a long-necked sea creature pursuing the depths of the loch. Several theories abound regarding what this creature may be. One says that Nessie could simply be a large dolphin or even a swimming elephant. Another says that perhaps she is a kind of plesiosaur, even though they went extinct millions of years ago. The only thing anyone knows for sure is that no one really knows what Nessie is. Nessie, and other mysterious creatures like her, are classified as *cryptics*. Cryptic creatures are creatures for which there is no empirical proof. In other words, no one can say with complete certainty that they exist. Big Foot and the Yeti, or Abominable Snowman, are also classified as cryptics. Of course, there are many others. There's the Fouke Monster, a kind of big hairy ape that reputedly lives in the swamps of Arkansas; or the infamous Jersey Devil, a flying demon who inhabits the Pine Barrens of New Jersey. The study of cryptic creatures is called *crytozoology*.

1. What is a loch?

   Ⓐ a river

   Ⓑ a lake

   Ⓒ an ocean

   Ⓓ a stream

2. Why is it unlikely that Nessie is a plesiosaur?

   Ⓔ She doesn't look like a plesiosaur.

   Ⓕ She is an elephant.

   Ⓖ Plesiosaurs are extinct.

   Ⓗ Plesiosaurs can't swim.

3. If there is no empirical proof of something it means that

   Ⓐ it can't be verified.

   Ⓑ it can be verified.

   Ⓒ it is completely false.

   Ⓓ it can't be classified.

4. Which of the following would a cryptozoologist study?

   Ⓔ a triceratops

   Ⓕ a mammal

   Ⓖ a demon duck

   Ⓗ sea creatures

Sudoku Puzzle

Directions: Each row, column, and 3 × 3 box should contain the numbers 1, 2, 3, 4, 5, 6, 7, 8, and 9. Fill in the blanks to complete the puzzle.

	5	9		6	2	1		7
2		6		3		5	9	4
7	1	3		9			6	2
5		2		7	8		4	1
8			3	4	1			
1	3		9	2		6		8
3	4					7	1	6
9	2	8		1		4		3
6		1		5		2	8	

Give It a Try! On graph paper or on a computer spreadsheet, try creating your own sudoku puzzle. Start with 81 squares, divided evenly into 9 rows and 9 columns. Further divide this into nine 3 × 3 boxes as above. Can you fill in all of your squares with the numbers 1–9 so that no number repeats within a row, column, or box?

Mean, Median, Mode

Directions: Read the descriptions for *mean*, *median*, and *mode*. Then, find the mean, median, and mode for each set of numbers. Round your answers to the nearest tenth.

- The **mean** (or average) is the sum of the values given divided by the total number of values given.

- The **median** is the middle value of an ordered set of values, or data. If the set of values contains an even number of values, then the median is the mean (average) of the two middle values.

- The **mode** is the number (value) or item (e.g., favorite flavor of ice cream) that appears most frequently in the data provided. There can be more than one mode.

1.
| 3 | 22 | 71 | 17 | 19 | 17 | 18 | 49 |

Mean: _____   Median: _____   Mode(s): _____

2.
| 189 | 229 | 108 | 542 | 229 | 256 | 199 | 108 |

Mean: _____   Median: _____   Mode(s): _____

3.
| 16 | 8 | 9 | 10 | 12 | 8 | 7 | 11 | 20 |

Mean: _____   Median: _____   Mode(s): _____

4.
| 1,029 | 1,021 | 1,872 | 1,332 | 1,222 | 2,872 | 1,872 | 1,116 |

Mean: _____   Median: _____   Mode(s): _____

5.
| 18 | 49.5 | 32.5 | 21 | 49.5 | 68.5 | 13 |

Mean: _____   Median: _____   Mode(s): _____

Homonyms

| **What to Know** | Homonyms are two or more words that have the same sound and often have similar spellings, but they have different meanings. |

Directions: Complete the sentences below. Choose from the homonyms in the box. Use each word only once.

accept	aloud	except	passed	peek	site
affect	cite	lessen	past	presence	taught
allowed	effect	lesson	peak	presents	taut

1. The teacher _____ her students how to properly _____ the sources they used in their research.

2. The climber kept the rope _____ as he made his way up to the mountain's

   _____.

3. Jo wanted to take a quick _____ at the _____ under the

   Christmas tree but she knew that wasn't _____.

4. Lou learned his _____ when everyone else _____ the class and he didn't.

5. The author announced his _____ and then proceeded to read

   _____ from his latest novel.

6. Coach told us that he could _____ the mistakes we made in the

   _____ as long as we learned from them.

7. All of us arrived at the _____ on time _____ for Pete, who was 20 minutes late.

8. Research showed that the healing _____ of the medicine could

   _____ in time, which would _____ the millions of patients who were taking it.

Inference

Directions: Read the story and then record facts that give you clues as to what Lena's job is. Finally, make an inference about what Lena's job is.

When Lena entered her office, she put down her briefcase and anxiously listened to her voicemail messages. She jotted down the phone numbers of the three people who called, grabbed her notebook and pen, and dialed the first number on her list. "Wow! Really? They found it in the backyard? Now, that's news!" she said. Lena asked the caller a series of questions and feverishly took notes as the person answered the questions. After making all of her calls, Lena began typing up the information she had gained. "This'll be great for the front page!" she exclaimed.

Clues — Name facts from the story that refer to the job that Lena is doing.

_____

_____

_____

_____

_____

_____

_____

Inference — State your conclusion about what Lena's job is. Explain why you came to this conclusion.

_____

_____

_____

_____

Greek Mythology

Directions: The ancient Greeks were polytheistic, which means that they worshipped more than one god. In fact, they believed in many gods. Use Greek mythology books or do online research to help you match the Greek gods and goddesses on the left to their descriptions on the right. Then, answer the questions below.

1. _____ Zeus

2. _____ Hera

3. _____ Poseidon

4. _____ Demeter

5. _____ Athena

6. _____ Hestia

7. _____ Aphrodite

8. _____ Apollo

9. _____ Ares

10. _____ Artemis

11. _____ Hephaestus

12. _____ Hermes

13. _____ Hades

14. _____ Dionysus

15. _____ Eros

A. He is the god of love.

B. She is the goddess of wisdom. She is the daughter of Zeus, and Athens is named for her.

C. He is the god of war and the son of Hera.

D. He is the king of the gods. He rules the thunder, rain, and lightning, among other things.

E. He is the god of wine and festivals.

F. She is the goddess of the home.

G. He is the god of the seas and the brother of Zeus. He lives at the bottom of the ocean and rules the waves.

H. He is the messenger of the gods.

I. He is the god of light and truth.

J. She is the goddess of the hunters and animals. She is the twin sister of Apollo.

K. She is the wife and sister of Zeus. She has a jealous streak and can be quite vengeful.

L. He is the god of the dead.

M. She is the goddess of agriculture.

N. He is the god of fire and volcanoes.

O. She is the goddess of beauty and love.

16. Name the place where the ancient Greeks believe these gods lived. _____

17. Name the famous sporting event originally held in honor of Zeus. _____

Sports Percentages

Directions: Write the expressions and calculate the percentages to solve each problem below. Use scratch paper to show your work. The first answer is given for you.

> **What to Know**
>
> 🥤 Shooting percentages in basketball are calculated by dividing the number of shots made by the number of attempted shots.
> 🥤 Passing percentages in football are calculated by dividing the number of completed passes by the number of attempted passes.
> 🥤 Winning percentages are calculated by dividing the number of games won by the total number of games played.
> 🥤 You need to add a decimal point and 2 or 3 zeroes to the dividend before dividing.

Problem	Equation	Answer
1. Your best basketball player attempted 20 shots and made 15. Calculate his shooting percentage.	15 ÷ 20 =	75%
2. A shooting guard on your school basketball team attempted 25 shots and made 18. What was the player's shooting percentage?		
3. The local school quarterback attempted 12 passes and completed 9 passes. What was the quarterback's passing percentage?		
4. The local school's soccer team played 10 games and won 6 games. What was the team's winning percentage?		
5. The local school's basketball team had a 24–game season and won 18 games. What was the team's winning percentage?		
6. The local school's football team played 10 games and won 8 games. What was its winning percentage?		
7. Joe is the quarterback of the intramural team. He attempts 25 passes and completes 16 passes. What is his passing percentage?		
8. The girls' softball team played 15 games and won 9 games. What is the team's winning percentage?		
9. The center on your basketball team attempted 40 shots and made 28 shots. What was the center's shooting percentage?		
10. The school baseball team played 28 games and won 21 games. What was its winning percentage?		

Persuasive Writing

In persuasive writing, the writer tries to get someone to agree with an idea or way of thinking.

Directions: Try your hand at persuasive writing by completing each list.

1. List three reasons why all students should wear school uniforms.

    a. _____

    b. _____

    c. _____

2. List three reasons why everyone should have a pet snake.

    a. _____

    b. _____

    c. _____

3. List three reasons why students should not have homework.

    a. _____

    b. _____

    c. _____

4. List three reasons why children should be allowed to vote in all major elections.

    a. _____

    b. _____

    c. _____

System Check

Directions: Match the job on the left with the body system on the right that is responsible for doing the job. Then, complete the statements at the bottom of the page.

Job

Body System

1. _____ Helps regulate body temperature

2. _____ Controls the body and carries messages

3. _____ Transports blood throughout the body

4. _____ Breaks down food to supply energy

5. _____ Takes in oxygen and removes carbon dioxide

6. _____ Produces new organisms

7. _____ Responsible for movement

8. _____ Eliminates waste in the form of urine

9. _____ Fights infections and disease

10. _____ Produces hormones that control body functions

11. _____ Supports the body and protects organs

A. Circulatory

B. Respiratory

C. Immune

D. Excretory

E. Muscular

F. Skeletal

G. Digestive

H. Endocrine

I. Nervous

J. Reproductive

K. Integumentary

12. The heart is part of the _____ system.

13. The spinal cord is part of the _____ system.

14. The pituitary gland is part of the _____ system.

15. The skin is part of the _____ system.

16. The femur is part of the _____ system.

17. Kidneys are part of the _____ system.

18. The large intestines are part of the _____ system.

Specialty Words

There are many words for specialized areas of study that end in *–ology*. The suffix *–ology* means "the science of" or "the study of" something. For example, geology is the study of Earth's crust. Many of these words are used when studying social studies and science.

Directions: Match the specialized areas with the definitions below.

— **-ology Words** —	**Definitions**
1. _____ meteorology	A. study of insects
2. _____ biology	B. study of fruit
3. _____ cytology	C. study of poisons
4. _____ dermatology	D. study of ancestors
5. _____ pomology	E. study of cells
6. _____ genealogy	F. study of life
7. _____ entomology	G. study of weather
8. _____ sociology	H. study of skin
9. _____ toxicology	I. study of society

Directions: Write the name of the specialist that matches the described field of study. You may use the words in the word box below to aid you.

10. An _____ studies about the eyes.

11. A _____ studies about newborn babies.

12. A _____ studies about criminal behavior.

13. An _____ studies about birds.

14. A _____ studies minerals.

15. A _____ studies the mind.

16. An _____ studies word origins.

17. A _____ studies living tissues.

mineralogist	criminologist	ornithologist	histologist
neonatologist	etymologist	ophthalmologist	psychologist

Ordering Decimals

Directions: Read each problem carefully. Fill in the answer circle that shows the given set of decimals ordered from **greatest to least.**

Sample

A. 0.3   2.039   0.390   0.391

- (A) 0.3   2.039   0.390   0.391
- (B) 2.039   0.391   0.390   0.3
- (C) 0.391   2.039   0.3   0.390
- (D) none of these

---

1.   2.79   2.079   2.1   2.709
- (A) 2.709   2.79   2.079   2.1
- (B) 2.1   2.079   2.79   2.709
- (C) 2.79   2.709   2.1   2.079
- (D) none of these

2.   0.5091   0.5901   0.0510   0.0051
- (E) 0.0051   0.0510   0.5901   0.5091
- (F) 0.5091   0.5901   0.0510   0.0051
- (G) 0.0051   0.0510   0.5901   0.5091
- (H) 0.5901   0.5091   0.0510   0.0051

3.   1.1   1.01   1.11   1.101
- (A) 1.11   1.101   1.1   1.01
- (B) 1.11   1.1   1.101   1.01
- (C) 1.1   1.101   1.11   1.01
- (D) none of these

4.   3.71   .207   .307   .3
- (E) .3   .307   .207   .371
- (F) 3.71   .307   .3   .207
- (G) .371   .3   .207   .307
- (H) none of these

5.   9.921   8.001   8.01   8.008
- (A) 8.001   8.01   8.008   9.921
- (B) 9.921   8.01   8.008   8.001
- (C) 8.01   9.921   8.001   8.008
- (D) 8.001   9.921   8.008   8.01

6.   0.21   0.0211   0.1201   0.1021
- (E) 0.0211   0.21   0.1201   0.1021
- (F) 0.1021   0.1201   0.0211   0.21
- (G) 0.21   0.0211   0.1021   0.1201
- (H) none of these

7.   0.007   0.017   0.0007   0.07
- (A) 0.07   0.017   0.007   0.0007
- (B) 0.0007   0.007   0.017   0.07
- (C) 0.007   0.07   0.017   0.0007
- (D) none of these

8.   2.3   0.310   2.402   1.317
- (E) 2.3   0.310   1.317   2.402
- (F) 1.317   2.402   0.310   2.3
- (G) 2.402   2.3   0.310   1.317
- (H) none of these

Complete Crossword

Directions: Complete this crossword puzzle with words that begin with *com*. Use the clues below.

Across

1. Did you shut down the _____ after you finished your online research?
2. The U.S. president is in _____ of all of the country's armed forces.
4. The new software _____ hired 10 workers this week.
7. After dinner, the chef would like to hear your _____ about the meal.
8. When asked to _____ an apple to an orange, he decided they had a lot in common.
9. The math problem was too _____ for me to solve without using a calculator.
11. Texts allow us to quickly _____ a thought to someone far away.

Down

1. The baker _____ the ingredients in a bowl before mixing them.
2. The hiker used a _____ to determine the direction she was heading.
3. You may not play video games until you _____ your homework.
5. Someone was causing a _____ by banging pots and pans together.
6. The neighbors formed a _____ in order to decide the best plan to clean up the park.
10. By taking a job closer to his home, he cut his morning _____ in half.

Excellent Exponents

What to Know

An exponent is used to show the number of times a base number is used as a factor. Rather than having to write $5 \times 5 \times 5 \times 5$, an exponent can be used. The value can be stated as 5^4.

Example: $5^4 = 5$ to the fourth power or $5 \times 5 \times 5 \times 5$

$5^4 = 625$

Part 1 Directions: The numbers below are written in exponential notation. Convert the numbers to the expanded form and then to standard form. The first one has been done for you.

1. 8^3 = _8 × 8 × 8 (expanded form)_ = _512_	2. 9^7 = _____ = _____
3. 15^4 = _____ = _____	4. 10^8 = _____ = _____
5. 6^6 = _____ = _____	6. 9^2 = _____ = _____

Part 2 Directions: Write each expression using an exponent. Find the product.

1. $6 \times 6 \times 6 \times 6 \times 6$ = _____ = _____	2. $7 \times 7 \times 7$ = _____ = _____
3. $2 \times 2 \times 2 \times 2$ = _____ = _____	4. $11 \times 11 \times 11 \times 11 \times 11$ = _____ = _____

The Escape Plan

Directions: Read the passage below and answer the questions that follow.

The rain was coming down so hard that Tilly felt as if she was going to drown. She was slopping through the mud and could feel her shoes sticking each time. She didn't have a coat, so she was beginning to shake uncontrollably. The blanket she had grabbed to wear was torn and ragged. It wasn't good for much.

Every muscle in Tilly's body ached with exhaustion. She had been on the road running for days now. She wasn't sure exactly how many days she had been gone because all of her running was done at night under the light of the moon. But tonight there was no moon: only the clouds that blocked the moonlight and her feeling of freedom. As long as the moon was in the sky, Tilly felt that she was safe and everything would be okay.

It all started when a new slave showed up on the plantation. She was assigned to work in the shed just outside the barn. But this new slave had also brought a plan—a plan for an escape. She was careful whom she shared the plan with, as it was dangerous to let too many people know. Tilly had listened to the plan, and she and her sister were resolute about going.

The escape route was dangerous and filled with fear. At any minute, a slave could be caught and returned to his or her owner to face the severe consequences of trying to run away.

1. Using the context clues, what does the word *resolute* mean as used in the third paragraph?

    A. determined

    B. intensified

    C. interrogated

    D. chided

2. What is the main idea of the last paragraph?

    A. to explain whether or not Tilly should trust the new slave

    B. to explain the dangers involved with the escape plan

    C. to explain the climax of the story

    D. to explain the resolution of the story

3. Using your background knowledge, what is the name of the escape route that Tilly will take to escape?

    A. The Freedom Train

    B. The Liberty Bell

    C. The Underground Railroad

    D. none of the above

Food Chains

Directions: Rearrange each list of organisms in a food chain in the correct order on the chart below. The first two have been done for you. Create two food chains of your own for numbers 9 and 10.

Chain #1	Chain #2	Chain #3	Chain #4
fox	plant plankton	lizard	lion
shrubs	bear	berries	grass
rabbit	salmon	grasshopper	antelope
	water snail		

Chain #5	Chain #6	Chain #7	Chain #8
snail	wolf	mink	great white shark
water plants	small plants	bark	clams
duck	vulture	hare	sea lions
great-horned owl	moose	great-horned owl	plankton

Reminders:

- Primary producers are plants.
- Primary consumers are plant eaters.
- Secondary consumers eat the plant eaters.
- Tertiary consumers are large and eat the smaller mammals and birds that are secondary consumers (and sometimes the primary consumers, too).

	Primary Producer	Primary Consumer	Secondary Consumer	Tertiary Consumer
Chain #1	shrubs	rabbit	fox	– – –
Chain #2	plant plankton	water snail	salmon	bear
Chain #3				
Chain #4				
Chain #5				
Chain #6				
Chain #7				
Chain #8				
Chain #9				
Chain #10				

Review the Basics

Directions: Correct the grammar, punctuation, capitalization, and spelling errors in the following sentences. If there are no errors in a sentence, leave the line blank.

1. your the First One in your famly, to have a bicycle of your verry own.

   _____

2. Jane Smith Kim Choi and Sitara Jaworski went too lakewood mall two by knew cloths!

   _____

3. Pedro won! _____

4. They was the verry last wons too leeve the room on valentine's day.

   _____

5. Are you the air to your wealthy Uncles estate.

   _____

6. we dont want too go to the party latter.

   _____

7. Jerry had his papier with him; but he didnt have his pencil?

   _____

8. Ari isn't never going shoping with them girls agin.

   _____

9. There is hardly any diffrences between them three girls.

   _____

10. On independence day wee had went to the Colorado river with are friends.

    _____

11. hurry, hurry! mother yelled. I need help with them groceries.

    _____

12. Mother asked us to hurry and to help her with the groceries.

    _____

Square Roots

What to Know

Some numbers have square roots that are whole numbers. The square root of a number is the number that when multiplied by itself will equal the first number given. There is a special symbol that is used to represent square root. The symbol $\sqrt{}$ is called the radical symbol.

Example: The square root of 81 is 9.

If you multiply 9 × 9, the answer is 81. So 9 multiplied by itself equals 81. Thus, 9 is the square root of 81.

$\sqrt{81}$ = 9

Directions: Find the square root of each number. Use a calculator for help if needed.

1. $\sqrt{16}$ = _____

2. $\sqrt{4,900}$ = _____

3. $\sqrt{169}$ = _____

4. $\sqrt{400}$ = _____

5. $\sqrt{64}$ = _____

6. $\sqrt{289}$ = _____

7. $\sqrt{25}$ = _____

8. $\sqrt{361}$ = _____

9. $\sqrt{841}$ = _____

10. $\sqrt{36}$ = _____

11. $\sqrt{225}$ = _____

12. $\sqrt{2,500}$ = _____

13. $\sqrt{2,025}$ = _____

14. $\sqrt{8,100}$ = _____

15. $\sqrt{490,000}$ = _____

16. $\sqrt{3,844}$ = _____

Popular Genres

Directions: Use the passage below to help answer each question.

Two popular fictional genres are fantasy and science fiction. Both fantasy and science fiction contain elements that seem unreal to the reader; however, many of the elements in science fiction are based on scientific discoveries the reader believes could happen in the future. For example, many science fiction stories involve space travel. People have already experienced space travel, so this seems possible to the reader even though the story might have people traveling and living on other planets, which has not happened. Fantasy involves more elements that are so fantastical the reader realizes they are not likely to happen. Fairies, dragons, monsters, and other supernatural creatures are often main characters in fantasy novels. Whether you like fantasy or science fiction better, both types of writing are wonderful reading entertainment.

1. Fantasy and science fiction are both fictional _____.

2. Explain how science fiction differs from fantasy. _____

   _____

   _____

3. Which of the two genres has more elements that are based on real-life experiences?

   _____

4. Which genre is more likely to have fairies, dragons, or other supernatural creatures?

   _____

5. Look in a library or do an online search (with an adult's permission) to find and list titles and authors of three fantasy books.

   a. _____

   b. _____

   c. _____

6. Think of a popular movie that is science fiction. What is the movie title?

   _____

   Research, if needed, and find out if the movie is based on a book. If so, what is the book title?

   _____

Hyperbole

What to Know

A *hyperbole* is a type of figurative language that shows an extreme exaggeration. A hyperbole helps create a better visual image for the reader. Creating a clearer image is what makes a hyperbole such an important part of figurative language.

Example: *Melanie's hair is so hard from all the hair spray she uses that her mother takes the hair left in the hairbrush and makes bricks for her walking path.*

Melanie's hair is really not hard enough to make bricks, but the hyperbole helps the reader imagine someone with hair that is extremely stiff from using too much hair spray.

Directions: Complete each statement to create a hyperbole of your own.

1. My mother is so nice that _____

_____

2. My little sister is so short that _____

_____

3. The teacher is so smart that _____

_____

4. His brother is so tall that _____

_____

5. The baby is so loud that _____

_____

6. The monster is so scary that _____

_____

7. Her smile is so big that _____

_____

8. The ocean is so deep that _____

_____

The Preamble

The writers of the United States Constitution wanted to strengthen national government and to secure peace for the United States. The Preamble of the Constitution states the purposes of this document. This is how the Preamble reads:

*We the people of the United States, in order to form a more perfect **union**, **establish** **justice**, **insure** domestic **tranquility**, provide for the common **defense**, **promote** the general **welfare**, and **secure** the blessings of liberty to ourselves and our **posterity**, do **ordain** and establish this Constitution for the United States of America.*

Directions: Below are definitions of the words shown in **bold** from the Preamble to the Constitution. Write the correct word next to its definition.

1. _____—"to contribute to the growth or prosperity"

2. _____—"to put beyond the hazard of losing"

3. _____—"to make certain by taking precautions"

4. _____—"formation of a single political unit from one or more separate individual units"

5. _____—"maintenance of what is just or morally upright and good"

6. _____—"the state of doing well in regard to happiness, well-being, or prosperity"

7. _____—"to establish by decree or law"

8. _____—"all further generations"

9. _____—"to organize and make firm or stable"

10. _____—"means or methods of protecting oneself"

11. _____—"relating to one's own country"

12. _____—"free from disturbance or turmoil"

Spelling Practice

Directions: Read each group of words carefully. Fill in the circle that has the underlined word spelled **incorrectly**. If all choices are correct, fill in "E."

Sample

Ⓐ volunteer <u>association</u>　　　Ⓑ your <u>suggestion</u>

Ⓒ <u>beneficial</u> treatment　　　⬤ real <u>explaination</u>　　　Ⓔ all correct

---

1. Ⓐ <u>foreign</u> country　　　Ⓑ barely <u>believable</u>
   Ⓒ very <u>disappointed</u>　　　Ⓓ <u>mischevous</u> cat　　　Ⓔ all correct

2. Ⓐ favorite <u>companion</u>　　　Ⓑ don't <u>interrupt</u>
   Ⓒ sign <u>languge</u>　　　Ⓓ became <u>necessary</u>　　　Ⓔ all correct

3. Ⓐ handsome <u>millionaire</u>　　　Ⓑ <u>ridiculous</u> idea
   Ⓒ <u>acceptable</u> procedure　　　Ⓓ <u>incredible</u> accuracy　　　Ⓔ all correct

4. Ⓐ old <u>equiptment</u>　　　Ⓑ <u>possessive</u> wife
   Ⓒ <u>leisure</u> time　　　Ⓓ general <u>admission</u>　　　Ⓔ all correct

5. Ⓐ <u>essential</u> supplies　　　Ⓑ close <u>attention</u>
   Ⓒ ancient <u>civlization</u>　　　Ⓓ nonprofit <u>organization</u>　　　Ⓔ all correct

6. Ⓐ earned <u>privilege</u>　　　Ⓑ <u>unkemt</u> room
   Ⓒ <u>dissatisfied</u> client　　　Ⓓ <u>misspelled</u> words　　　Ⓔ all correct

7. Ⓐ dangerous <u>intersetion</u>　　　Ⓑ <u>communicate</u> often
   Ⓒ large <u>mortgage</u>　　　Ⓓ <u>military</u> action　　　Ⓔ all correct

8. Ⓐ Islamic <u>religion</u>　　　Ⓑ <u>hideous</u> sight
   Ⓒ not <u>knowlegeable</u>　　　Ⓓ <u>irresponsible</u> decision　　　Ⓔ all correct

9. Ⓐ <u>persuasive</u> person　　　Ⓑ faulty <u>judgment</u>
   Ⓒ jazz <u>musician</u>　　　Ⓓ happens <u>occasionally</u>　　　Ⓔ all correct

10. Ⓐ <u>influential</u> speech　　　Ⓑ unclear <u>description</u>
    Ⓒ wrong <u>pronunciation</u>　　　Ⓓ <u>seperate</u> rooms　　　Ⓔ all correct

11. Ⓐ U.S. <u>Constitution</u>　　　Ⓑ <u>miscellanious</u> stuff
    Ⓒ <u>unmistakable</u> odor　　　Ⓓ <u>distinct</u> personality　　　Ⓔ all correct

12. Ⓐ employees' <u>committee</u>　　　Ⓑ still <u>self-sufficient</u>
    Ⓒ great <u>courage</u>　　　Ⓓ <u>temporary</u> lodgings　　　Ⓔ all correct

---

A Name Game

Directions: See if you can solve this riddle!

> Cathy's mother, Mrs. Gutierrez, had exactly four children. The oldest, a girl, she named "Left." The second oldest, a boy, she named "Right." The third child, also a girl, was named "Up." The youngest child was also a girl. What was her name?

Use the work area below to chart this problem. Record your answer at the bottom of the page.

Work Area

1st Child	2nd Child	3rd Child	4th Child

Positive & Negative

Directions: Solve the addition and subtraction problems. Remember that subtracting a negative is the same as adding a positive.

1. 3 + (–61) = _____

2. –6 + (–7) = _____

3. 18 + (–18) = _____

4. 34 – (–6) = _____

5. –22 + (–14) = _____

6. –77 + (–19) = _____

7. 54 – (–13) = _____

8. 2 + (–12) = _____

9. –13 – 7 = _____

10. 51 + (–62) = _____

Directions: Solve the multiplication and division problems.

What to Know

- A negative times a negative is a positive.
- A positive times a negative is a negative.
- A negative divided by a negative is a positive.
- A positive divided by a negative is a negative.
- A negative divided by a positive is negative.

11. –7 × (–7) = _____

12. –12 × (–10) = _____

13. –8 × 7 = _____

14. 18 × (–7) = _____

15. –45 ÷ (–15) = _____

16. 112 ÷ 4 = _____

17. 49 ÷ (–7) = _____

18. –24 ÷ 4 = _____

19. 14 × (–4) = _____

20. –108 ÷ (–9) = _____

Connotation & Denotation

What to Know

In writing, there are two different kinds of meanings of the words you use. The *denotation* of a word is the meaning that you would find in the dictionary. The *connotation* of a word is the feeling or mental picture that people associate with the word.

For example, the words "notorious" and "famous" have different connotations. "Notorious" has a negative connotation. It makes you think that a person is well known for bad or outrageous things. "Famous" suggests that a person is well known for doing good and wonderful things.

Directions: Label each word by writing either "positive" or "negative" to describe its connotation.

1. _____ quickly/hastily _____

2. _____ debate/argument _____

3. _____ odor/fragrance _____

4. _____ snoop/investigate _____

5. _____ attract/lure _____

6. _____ call/yell _____

Directions: For each of the following words, write a word that has a similar denotation but has a different connotation. Feel free to use a thesaurus for this activity.

7. mistake _____

8. revere _____

9. regretful _____

10. mend _____

11. melt _____

12. pizzazz _____

Directions: Create your own lists of words with positive and negative connotations.

Positive	Negative
_____	_____
_____	_____
_____	_____
_____	_____

Symbol of Freedom

Directions: Read the story and poem aloud. Context clues can help to derive meaning from this poem. Use the context clues in the poem to answer the questions.

The Statue of Liberty was a gift from France to the United States. President Grover Cleveland dedicated the Statue of Liberty. It was unveiled before representatives from France and the United States. The Statue of Liberty is a symbol of welcome for many immigrants. A poem written by Emma Lazarus is inscribed on the statue's pedestal. It reads as follows:

Not like the brazen giant of Greek fame,
  With conquering limbs astride from land to land;
  Here at sea-washed, sunset gates shall stand
A mighty woman with a torch, whose flame
Is the imprisoned lightning, and her name
  Mother of Exiles. From her beacon-hand
  Glows world-wide welcome; her mild eyes command
The air-bridged harbor that twin cities frame.
"Keep ancient lands, your storied pomp!" cries she
  With silent lips. "Give me your tired, your poor,
Your huddled masses yearning to breathe free,
  The wretched refuse of your teeming shore.
Send these, the homeless, tempest-tost to me,
  I lift my lamp beside the golden door!"

1. Who is the "Mother of Exiles"? _____

2. Name three descriptions of the Statue of Liberty from the poem. _____

_____

3. Define the following words:

   brazen _____

   beacon _____

   astride _____

   yearning _____

4. How does the poem describe those whom the Statue of Liberty is there to inspire?

_____

Checks & Balances

The delegates to the Constitutional Convention knew that a strong central government was important, but they did not want to give any one person too much control. That's why they established a system of checks and balances in our government. The United States Constitution, which defines the powers of the government, established three distinct branches of government: executive, legislative, and judicial. Each branch has its own distinct powers and the ability to limit the powers of the other branches. This system of checks and balances disperses power among the three branches of government and prevents one branch from having too much power.

Directions: Write a brief description of each branch of government and at least one way it can limit the power of another branch.

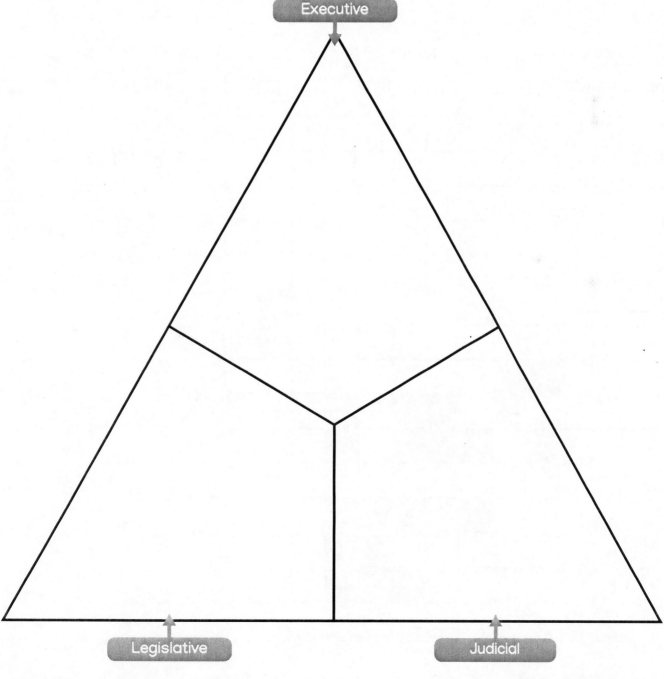

Algebraic Equations

Directions: Find the value of the missing integer (*y*) in each equation. Then, write each answer as a number word in the number puzzle. See #2 Across. It has been done for you.

— Across —

2. 1y – 3 = 27   y = <u>30</u>

3. 7y + 9 = 37   y = _____

6. 3y – 5 = 25   y = _____

7. 3y + 8 = 35   y = _____

8. 9 + 2y = 17   y = _____

10. 3y + 9 = 63   y = _____

11. 4y + 4 = 24   y = _____

13. 4y – 1 = 63   y = _____

15. 3 + 5y = 23   y = _____

16. 8y – 4 = 52   y = _____

17. 8y – 8 = 16   y = _____

— Down —

1. 6y – 8 = 22   y = _____

2. 6y – 3 = 15   y = _____

4. 9 + 2y = 41   y = _____

5. 5y – 9 = 26   y = _____

6. 5y + 2 = 17   y = _____

8. 8y + 1 = 41   y = _____

9. 7y – 6 = 15   y = _____

11. 2y – 26 = 74   y = _____

12. 1y + 7 = 16   y = _____

14. 7 + 4y = 87   y = _____

15. 9 + 5y = 34   y = _____

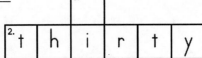

Setting the Mood

Directions: Choose one of the following moods. Circle that mood and then create a setting that would develop that mood. Write a description of your setting on the lines below. Remember to include a "where" and a "when" and to use as many details as you can. In the box below, draw a picture of your setting.

scary   mysterious   excited   pleasant   sad   funny

_____

_____

_____

_____

_____

_____

_____

Types of Energy

Directions: Define renewable and nonrenewable energy sources, then label the pictures as renewable or nonrenewable. Write your response to the question at the bottom of the page.

Renewable energy sources

_____

_____

Nonrenewable energy sources

_____

_____

1. _____	2. _____
3. COAL _____	4. _____

Which type of energy source is better for the environment? Give three reasons to support your opinion.

_____

_____

_____

Yes or No?

Directions: Read each pair of sentences. If the italicized sentence is correct, based on the first sentence, write **yes.** If the italicized sentence is not correct, write **no.**

		Yes or No?
1.	Janelle was whimpering when she arrived home. *She was laughing.*	
2.	The detective unraveled the mystery. *He solved the mystery.*	
3.	The author's autobiography was thorough. *It was a detailed account.*	
4.	Because she owed Timothy a favor, Marcella felt obliged to contribute to the fund. *Marcella felt compelled to give to the fund.*	
5.	A suit is usually acceptable attire for a job interview. *A suit is usually inappropriate attire for a job interview.*	
6.	At their friend's birthday party, Josefina mocked Consuela. *Josefina ridiculed Consuela.*	
7.	The puppies were ideal companions for the sick child. *They were perfect companions for the sick child.*	
8.	Jason decided not to deceive his parents. *He decided to be truthful.*	
9.	The prizewinning photographer was an amateur. *The prizewinning photographer was a professional.*	
10.	Blackhawk is a distinguished leader of his tribe. *Blackhawk is a significant tribal leader.*	
11.	My mother allowed my slumber to continue until noon. *She let me sleep until noon.*	
12.	We detested the opera performance. *We enjoyed the opera.*	
13.	Mary and Jane debated about leaving. *They agreed it was time to leave.*	
14.	Alexander was always able to conceal his emotions. *He always openly displayed his emotions.*	

Evaluating Expressions

Directions: Read each problem carefully. Fill in the correct answer circle.

Samples

Let $p = 7$ and $r = 9$

A. $p - 3$

Ⓐ 2   ● 4
Ⓑ 3   Ⓓ $\frac{1}{5}$

B. $r \times 7$

Ⓔ 0   Ⓖ 60
● 63   Ⓗ none of those

Let $m = 10$ and $y = 8$

1. $25 - m$

Ⓐ 10   Ⓒ 51
Ⓑ 15   Ⓓ 35

5. $m \div 5$

Ⓐ 15   Ⓒ 0
Ⓑ 12   Ⓓ 2

2. $\frac{y}{2}$

Ⓔ 2   Ⓖ 4
Ⓕ 8   Ⓗ 16

6. $3y + 9$

Ⓔ 24   Ⓖ 94
Ⓕ 32   Ⓗ 33

3. $17m$

Ⓐ 107   Ⓒ 170
Ⓑ 27   Ⓓ none of these

7. $\frac{m}{5} - 2$

Ⓐ 0   Ⓒ 2
Ⓑ 48   Ⓓ none of these

4. my

Ⓔ 18   Ⓖ 80
Ⓕ 2   Ⓗ 8

8. $m - 13y$

Ⓔ 94   Ⓖ 2
Ⓕ 1.3   Ⓗ −94

Telephone Tag

Directions: For many years, people have used coded languages in order to communicate. Some familiar coded languages are Morse code and sign language. For this activity, we will be using the telephone for a coded language.

Each number on the telephone is associated with three to four letters. You may need to experiment a few times before you find the right letter. Use the telephone code below to help you decipher the messages at the bottom of the page.

1—no letters	6—M, N, O
2—A, B, C	7—P (Q), R, S
3—D, E, F	8—T, U, V
4—G, H, I	9—W, X, Y, (Z)
5—J, K, L	0—no letters

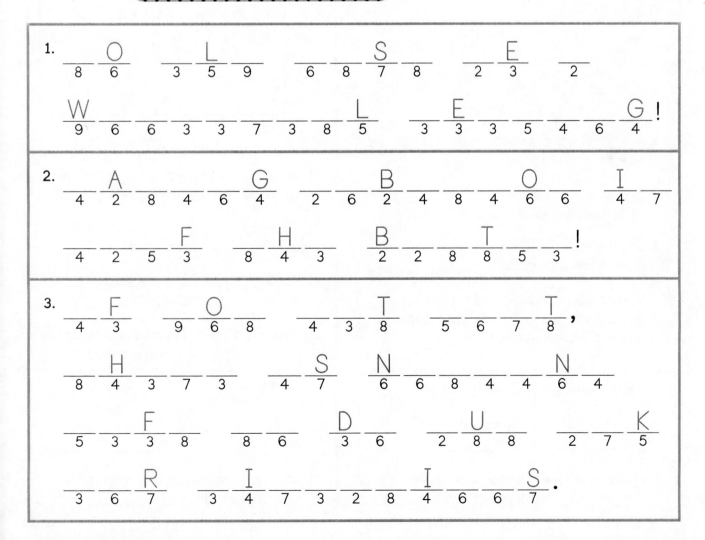

1.
```
 _  O      _  L  _      _  _  S  _     _  E  _
 8  6      3  5  9      6  8  7  8     2  3  2

 W  _  _  _  _  _  _  _  L      _  E  _  _  _  _  _  G !
 9  6  6  3  3  7  3  8  5      3  3  3  5  4  6  4
```

2.
```
 _  A  _  _  G  _     _  _  B  _  _  O  _     _  I  _
 4  2  8  4  6  4     2  6  2  4  8  4  6  6  4  7

 _  _  _  F  _     _  H  _     _  B  _  _  T  _ !
 4  2  5  3        8  4  3     2  2  8  8  5  3
```

3.
```
 _  F  _     _  O  _     _  _  T     _  _  _  T ,
 4  3        9  6  8     4  3  8     5  6  7  8

 _  H  _  _  _     _  S  _  N  _  _  _  N  _
 8  4  3  7  3     4  7  6  6  8  4  4  6  4

 _  F  _  _     _  _     _  D  _     _  U  _     _  _  K
 5  3  3  8     8  6     3  6        2  8  8     2  7  5

 _  _  R     _  I  _  _     _  I  _     _  S .
 3  6  7     3  4  7  3     2  8  4  6  6  7
```

Reading Graphs

Directions: Look at the graphs, then answer the related questions.

This single line graph illustrates the percentage of children in the general population from 1950 until 2000. Study the graph and use the information to answer the questions below.

Population of Children in the U.S.

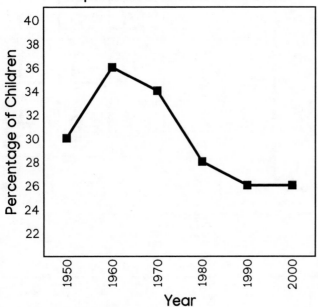

1. In which year did children comprise 36% of the population? _____

2. In which years were only 26% of the population children? _____

3. What year saw the highest percentage of children? _____

4. In which ten–year period did the number of children as a percentage of the population rise? _____

5. In which years are children just about one–fourth of the population? _____

6. In which ten–year period did the greatest drop occur? _____

7. In which ten–year period were children more than one third of the population? _____

This double line graph shows the average heights of boys and girls by age from 7 through 16. Study the graph and answer the questions below.

Average Heights of Children

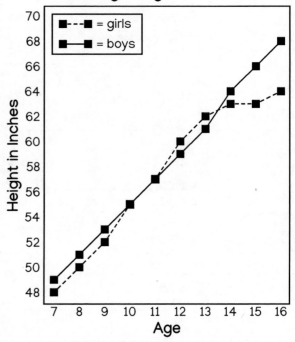

8. At which two ages do boys and girls average the same heights? _____

9. At which two ages are girls on average taller than boys? _____

10. At what age do boys average 4 inches taller than girls? _____

11. At what three ages do boys and girls grow at about the same amount before the girls catch up to boys?

    _____

12. Are 12-year-old girls usually taller or shorter than boys? _____

13. At what age do boys catch up and then pass girls? _____

The Fall

Directions: Read the passage below and answer the questions that follow.

Brett cinched his rope a little tighter around his waist and **maneuvered** his left foot into his next hold position. The sun was beating down on his neck.

"How are you doing down there?" called Evan from up above.

"Doing well, thanks," replied Brett.

Evan had been teaching Brett how to rappel and rock–climb all summer long. Evan had been doing it for years. The exhilaration that came from being at the top of the mountain or rock was worth more than the risk for Brett. But he knew that any minute, a rope could slip and he could be injured.

Evan continued to climb higher and in the process sent a few small rocks down on Brett. Brett closed his eyes to avoid getting hit. As he opened his eyes he heard a loud yell and he saw Evan's body flash in front of him.

"Oh, no!" thought Brett. "Evan has fallen."

Brett froze and didn't know what to do next. He could still hear Evan yelling, so he knew that was a good sign. Brett heard Evan smash up against something. At least he had broken his fall. Nothing but silence came from below.

"Hey Ev?" asked Brett. "Are you okay?"

"Uhhhhhh," moaned Evan. "My leg and my shoulder."

Brett knew that he had to get down and help Evan. He was scared. Thoughts of Evan's instructions went through his mind. Brett inched his way down closer and closer to Evan. He could still hear Evan moaning. Oh, if he could just go faster!

1. Which words best describe how Brett was feeling at the beginning of the passage?

    a. hesitant and concentrating
    b. happy and content
    c. relieved and tired
    d. stressed and overwhelmed

2. Which sentence explains the main problem in the story?

    a. Brett's an expert rock climber.
    b. Brett is worried that he won't be as good as Evan.
    c. Evan has fallen and needs Brett's help.
    d. Brett doesn't know how to rock–climb.

3. What is the meaning of the word *maneuvered* as used in the passage?

    a. driven   b. woke   c. moved   d. realized

Isaac Newton

Directions: Read the passage and answer the questions that follow.

Isaac Newton was an **innovator.** He lived from 1642–1727 and made some of the most important discoveries in the history of science. He completely changed the way Earth and the entire universe were understood by scientists. At the age of 23, Newton discovered a major concept in algebra, which was then a new kind of math. At the same age, he worked out the basic ideas of calculus. This is a kind of math important to space travel and to understanding the size and nature of space. We couldn't even put a person in space without the figures made possible by this kind of math!

Newton also discovered the basic law of gravity. This is the idea that all objects in the universe are pulled toward each other. It explains that the strength of this pull depends on the mass of each object. The force also depends on how far away objects are from each other. More massive objects have greater power to pull other objects. And objects closer to each other have a greater power to pull. Newton explained the three laws of motion. These laws describe the actions of moving objects and how other forces affect these objects. All of his ideas help explain the nature of matter and energy.

Newton was the first scientist to prove that white light itself is made up of seven colors. They are red, orange, yellow, green, blue, indigo, and violet. He also invented the reflecting telescope. This improved tool made possible a much more detailed study of the stars and planets. In the minds of many people, Isaac Newton is the greatest scientist of all time.

1. From the context of the passage, what does *innovator* mean?

   a. someone who plays with objects   **c.** someone who likes math

   b. someone who studies colors   **d.** someone who makes changes

2. Which of the following would be the most likely use of calculus?

   a. to compute the interest owed on a small debt

   b. to determine the amount of force needed to escape Earth's atmosphere in a rocket

   c. to compute the amount of gas needed to travel 500 miles in a car

   d. both b and c

3. Which of the following statements can you infer relate to the laws of motion?

   a. An unmoving object will remain unmoving until acted upon by an outside force.

   b. A moving object may speed up or slow down depending upon the force applied to the object.

   c. How much an object is affected by a force will depend upon the size and weight of the object.

   d. all of the above

4. Which of the following discoveries by Newton do not relate in some way to space, the universe, or planets?

   a. the law of gravity   **b.** calculus   **c.** laws of motion   **d.** none of the above

Semicolons

What to Know	A **semicolon** links two short, related sentences to make a longer sentence. Both of these sentences must have a subject and a predicate before you can link them with a semicolon. Use semicolons to add variety to your writing.

Examples: I like to cook; yesterday, I made dinner for my family.
Swifts are fascinating birds; they nest in chimneys and catch bugs in midair.
We're driving to the snow; we'd better make sure we have chains on our car.

Directions: Study the pairs of sentences below. If they are related, rewrite them as one long sentence, using a semicolon. If they are not related, leave them as is and write "not related."

1. Frida Kahlo is a famous artist. She lived in Mexico and painted pictures.

   _____

2. I'm Kellie's best friend. She always invites me to her birthday parties.

   _____

3. Nisha has always wanted to see Australia. Aphids are taking over Mom's roses.

   _____

4. Pablo cannot stop coughing. His father has gone to buy cough syrup.

   _____

5. Some say to apply butter to a burned area on the body. This is not a good idea.

   _____

6. I need to get glasses. That candle set fire to the curtain.

   _____

7. When handling the American flag, never let it touch the ground. This shows respect for the flag.

   _____

8. My older brother got a job at a shoe store. Broccoli is not my favorite vegetable.

   _____

Directions: Study the following run-on sentences. Add a semicolon to fix them.

9. Richard Bach wrote about seagulls, later, he wrote about airplanes.

10. *Metamorphosis* is a book by Franz Kafka it's about a man who turns into a bug.

11. Chickens make wonderful pets, they'll even come when you call them.

12. Driving on Route 66 is exciting you never know what you'll see.

13. The wedding was postponed the bride and groom were ill with the flu.

14. They put their house up for sale, they're moving to Alaska.

Circumference

What to Know

- The circumference is the distance around a circle.
- Pi = 3.14. The symbol for pi is π.
- To find the circumference, multiply 3.14 times the diameter. $C = \pi d$
- To find the circumference, multiply 2 times the radius times 3.14. $C = 2\pi r$

Directions: Compute the circumference for each circle below.

1. 10 ft.

C= _____

2. 20 cm

C= _____

3. 7 ft.

C= _____

4. 11 in.

C= _____

5. 8 m

C= _____

6. 15 cm

C= _____

7. 18 ft.

C= _____

8. 40 yds.

C= _____

9. 16 m

C= _____

10. 80 mm

C= _____

76

Vocabulary in Context

Directions: Read the following speech of a blackbird to a scarecrow. Find the meaning of each underlined word. Put the letter of the answer on the blank line. Use the definitions in the box below to help you.

A. bother, annoy	C. grouchy, grumpy	E. guard, protector
B. a silly trick	D. stick out	F. make a forward move

1. _____

2. _____

3. _____

4. _____

5. _____

6. _____

Caw! Caw! Caw! What's that ugly thing doing in my cornfield? You don't suppose that is what they call a scarecrow? Huh! Well, it doesn't scare me! Hey, you ¹<u>ornery</u> thing! Stop waving your long arms around my face. That's my corn, you know. You can stop your ²<u>caper</u> right now, and let me get my lunch! In fact, you are really beginning to ³<u>irk</u> me. So, stop waving around like that. I'm about to ⁴<u>lunge</u> at you and bite you if I don't get my lunch soon. Anyway, why does all of your hair ⁵<u>protrude</u> like that? Haven't you heard of a comb? Now, here I come! You might think you are a ⁶<u>sentinel</u>, but my desire for corn is stronger than my fear of you!

Directions: Circle the best answer to each of the following questions.

7. Which would be another name for a watchdog?   caper   sentinel

8. What do you call it when something irritates you?   sentinels   irks

9. Which might make you laugh?   caper   ornery

10. Which word describes a sudden pounce?   ornery   lunge

11. What describes a bad attitude?   protrude   ornery

12. What is another word for when something extends beyond a surface?   protrude   irk

Directions: Use each new word in a sentence.

13. _____

14. _____

15. _____

16. _____

17. _____

18. _____

Go There

Directions: Is there some place that you have always wanted to visit? Imagine that you are entering a contest to win a trip to one of the destinations listed in the box. To enter, you must write a one-paragraph letter that explains why you want to go there. Include in your letter three reasons why you want to make your visit.

Bahamas	Hawaii	Legoland	Seattle, WA
Bermuda	Holland	London, England	Paris, France
Disneyland	Jamaica	Los Angeles, CA	Tahiti
Disney World	India	Montreal, Canada	Washington, D.C.
Germany	Ireland	Rome, Italy	Melbourne, Australia
Greece	Japan	Scotland	Rio de Janeiro, Brazil

Dear Contest Judges,

    I would like to go to _____ because

_____

_____

_____

_____

_____

_____

_____

_____

_____

                        Sincerely Yours,

_____

The First Thirteen

What to Know	On May 29, 1790, Rhode Island became the last of the original 13 U.S. states to ratify the U.S. Constitution.

Directions: The names of those first 13 states are hidden in the box below. Do the following:

- Find and circle the names of states 2–13.

- Write the names of the states in the order in which they ratified the U.S. Constitution.

- Highlight the letters in the name of the first state to ratify the Constitution. (Hint: Once you have found and circled states 2–13, put the first 8 uncircled letters in order to spell the name of the 1st state.)

```
D E A I N A V L Y S N N E P
C N E W H A M P S H I R E L
A O W R H O D E I S L A N D
A A N I L O R A C H T R O N
R E L N I A V G E O R G I A
N E W J E R S E Y P H O U L
S O U T H C A R O L I N A Y
R G N I R A T M S P N A L R
M Z C A I R V I R G I N I A
W S T T E S U H C A S S A M
L E C W E D F N E U L R G I
I J K R O Y W E N W T K U A
```

Write the names of the states here:

13th: _____   6th: _____

12th: _____   5th: _____

11th: _____   4th: _____

10th: _____   3rd: _____

9th: _____   2nd: _____

8th: _____   1st: _____

7th: _____

Synonyms

Directions: Look at the underlined word in each sentence. Find a synonym for that word. Fill in the correct answer circle.

Sample

Not everyone <u>enjoyed</u> his performance.

Ⓐ disliked   Ⓒ hated

🅑 liked   Ⓓ sad

---

1. After I <u>finished</u> my math homework, I ran an errand for my mother.
   Ⓐ destroyed
   Ⓑ completed
   Ⓒ studied
   Ⓓ copied

2. The film was so frightening that <u>several</u> people had to leave the cinema!
   Ⓓ few
   Ⓕ scared
   Ⓖ many
   Ⓗ theatre

3. The view from the top of the building was <u>spectacular</u>.
   Ⓐ disappointing
   Ⓑ obstructed
   Ⓒ boring
   Ⓓ amazing

4. Some reptiles can be very <u>aggressive</u> if they feel threatened.
   Ⓔ calm
   Ⓕ fearful
   Ⓖ combative
   Ⓗ quick

5. The food at the party was <u>delicious</u>.
   Ⓐ tasty
   Ⓑ nasty
   Ⓒ salty
   Ⓓ none of these

6. It's a good idea to be <u>cautious</u> when you cross the street at a busy intersection.
   Ⓔ reckless
   Ⓕ terrified
   Ⓖ happy
   Ⓗ careful

7. The weather was so <u>dreadful</u>, the carnival had to be cancelled.
   Ⓐ beautiful
   Ⓑ rainy
   Ⓒ awful
   Ⓓ hot

8. I wanted to buy the shoes, but they were just too <u>expensive</u>.
   Ⓔ pricey
   Ⓕ cheap
   Ⓖ small
   Ⓗ ugly

In Other Words

Directions: Have you ever heard of the story "Feline Wearing Galoshes"? How about "Puss in Boots"? You might be surprised at how using different synonyms (words that have similar meanings) to describe a story you've heard before makes it sound very different. Try using synonyms to decipher the following well-known fairy tales and nursery rhymes. If you are not sure what some of the words mean, look them up in a dictionary or thesaurus. The first one has been done for you.

1. Ovoid Individual Mortally Injured in Fall

   Humpty Dumpty

2. Serious Overcrowding Discovered in Unique Foot-Based Dwelling

3. Remote Country Animal Home Vandalized by Hungry, Tired Girl

4. Rain or Shine, Tiny Arachnid Scales Pipe

5. Musical Feline, Amused Canine Witness Lunar Leap

6. Rural Homemaker Terrorized by Trio of Sightless Rodents

7. Elderly Farmer Lives with Many Noisy Animals

8. Lovely Somnambulist Wakened by Royal Kiss

Mystery Angles

Directions: Compute the number of degrees in each unmarked angle.

What to Know

The sum of the interior angles of every triangle is 180°.
The interior angles of a quadrilateral always add up to 360°.

1. 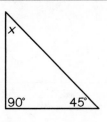 x = _____	**2.** 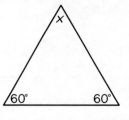 x = _____	**3.** 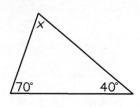 x = _____
4. 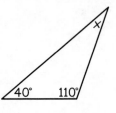 x = _____	**5.** 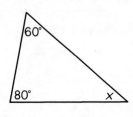 x = _____	**6.** 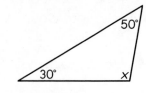 x = _____
7. 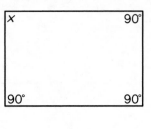 x = _____	**8.** 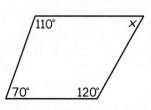 x = _____	**9.** 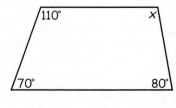 x = _____
10. 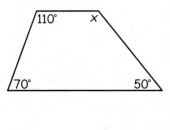 x = _____	**11.** 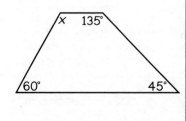 x = _____	**12.** 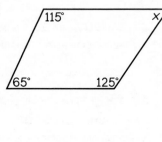 x = _____

Choose Wisely

What to Know There are some words that are often used incorrectly. They are paired here because they are often used interchangeably, but they are words that cannot be substituted for one another without changing the meaning of the sentence or making it nonsensical.

Example: The word *reign* means "to rule," while the word *rein* means "to control or guide."

Correct Uses: The king *reigned* for a long time. His advisors could not *rein* him in when he tried to start a war.

Directions: Choose the correct word to complete the sentence and write it on the line. You may need to refer to a dictionary.

1. **(affect/effect)** If you don't get enough sleep, it could _____ your ability to think clearly.

2. **(beside/besides)** No one sat _____ us at the concert, so we had plenty of space.

3. **(accept/except)** The teacher said he will not _____ any assignments turned in late.

4. **(council/counsel)** Dentists have to _____ their patients about proper hygiene.

5. **(farther/further)** How much _____ did you jog today than yesterday?

6. **(precede/proceed)** Once my phone is recharged, we can _____ with this conversation.

7. **(principal/principle)** I'm proud to say that the _____ has never had to call me into her office.

8. **(advise/advice)** The counselor gave good _____ for how to address my issue with Kay.

9. **(aisle/isle)** It's considered a fire hazard to block an _____ in a movie theater.

10. **(a lot/allot)** How much money did the committee _____ for advertising?

11. **(lose/loose)** We had to stop twice to tighten the _____ ropes.

12. **(later/latter)** Instead of choosing the former option, Ty chose the _____ one instead.

13. **(moral/morale)** Coach's halftime speech boosted the team's _____ and led to the win.

14. **(Who's/Whose)** _____ volunteering to deliver the pizza to that haunted house?

News Report

Directions: Find and read a news article in a newspaper or online about a world event. Then answer the following questions about what you read. Use complete sentences.

What is the headline? _____

_____

What is the article about? _____

_____

_____

When did the event happen? _____

Where did the event take place? _____

Who was involved in the event? _____

_____

_____

Why did the event occur? _____

_____

_____

List three words from the article that you are not familiar with. Look them up in a dictionary, and write down what they mean.

1 _____

2 _____

3 _____

What else would you like to know about the event? _____

_____

_____

_____

_____

_____

84

The Electoral College

Directions: Read the article. Circle the letter beside the best answer to each question below.

In spite of its name, the Electoral College is not a college. It is a group of people chosen in each state. The writers of the Constitution did not agree on how a president should be chosen. Some did not trust ordinary people to make a good choice. So they compromised. They agreed to have the Electoral College do it. Each state has a number of electors equal to its number of U.S. House members plus two. The District of Columbia also has three electoral votes. In the early days electors voted for whomever they wanted.

Now the political parties hold primary elections and conventions. They choose candidates for president and vice president. When voters pick the candidate of a particular party, they are actually choosing electors from that party. These electors have agreed to vote for their party's candidate. Except in very rare cases, this is what they do.

In almost all states, the party that gets the most votes in November wins all the electoral votes for the state. The electors meet in state capitals in December. In January, the electors' votes are opened. This happens in a special session of Congress. What if no candidate wins a majority of these votes? Then the House of Representatives chooses the president. This happened two times during the 1800s.

1. The Electoral College exists because
    a. it is where people go to learn how to be politicians.
    b. some of the Constitution's writers didn't think average people could make a presidential choice.
    c. George Washington insisted on having it as a safeguard.
    d. once people vote for a president, the College must decide on a vice president.

2. The Electoral College meets to vote in
    a. January.
    b. July.
    c. November.
    d. December.

3. The number of electors for each state is
    a. two more than its number of House Representatives.
    b. the same as the number of senators for that state.
    c. three.
    d. five.

Identifying Angles

Directions: Use the graphics to answer each set of questions.

What to Know
- 🥤 Adjacent angles are next to each other on a transversal.
- 🥤 Adjacent angles are supplementary. They add up to 180°.
- 🥤 Corresponding angles are in the same position on different lines.
- 🥤 Corresponding angles are congruent. They are the same size.

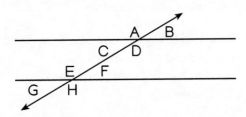

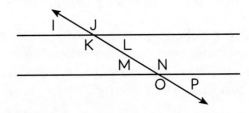

1. Name the eight pairs of adjacent angles.

Angle ___A___ and Angle ___B___

Angle _____ and Angle _____

Angle _____ and Angle _____

Angle _____ and Angle _____

Angle _____ and Angle _____

Angle _____ and Angle _____

Angle _____ and Angle _____

Angle _____ and Angle _____

2. Name the four pairs of corresponding angles.

Angle ___B___ and Angle ___F___

Angle _____ and Angle _____

Angle _____ and Angle _____

Angle _____ and Angle _____

3. Compute the measurement of each angle.

Angle A = ___150°___   Angle E = _____

Angle B = _____   Angle F = _____

Angle C = _____   Angle G = _____

Angle D = _____   Angle H = _____

4. Name the eight pairs of adjacent angles.

Angle _____ and Angle _____

Angle _____ and Angle _____

Angle _____ and Angle _____

Angle _____ and Angle _____

Angle _____ and Angle _____

Angle _____ and Angle _____

Angle _____ and Angle _____

Angle _____ and Angle _____

5. Name the four pairs of corresponding angles.

Angle _____ and Angle _____

Angle _____ and Angle _____

Angle _____ and Angle _____

Angle _____ and Angle _____

6. Compute the measurement of each angle.

Angle I = ___30°___   Angle M = _____

Angle J = _____   Angle N = _____

Angle K = _____   Angle O = _____

Angle L = _____   Angle P = _____

Here's How

Directions: Think about something you do very well. Use the template below to write a how–to paragraph explaining how you do it.

It is very easy to _____, and I will tell you how I do it.

First, I _____

_____

_____

_____

Next, I _____

_____

_____

_____

_____

After that, I _____

_____

_____

_____

_____

_____

Finally, I _____

_____

_____

_____

And now you know that it is easy to _____

_____

The Pull of Gravity

Directions: Read the passage below. Then imagine a person who weighs 90 pounds on Earth. Multiply that person's weight times the surface gravity of each planet to determine how much they would weigh there. Record your findings on the lines provided.

Example: 100 pounds × 0.38 surface gravity = 38 pounds (weight on Mercury)

After you have completed your calculations, answer the questions at the bottom of the page.

Gravity is the invisible force that pulls one object toward another object. The mass of an object determines the strength of its gravitational pull. An object with a large amount of mass exerts more gravitational force than an object with less mass.

When you step on a scale, it measures how powerfully Earth's gravity is pulling on you. Therefore, although your mass remains the same, your weight will vary depending on where you are in space because the surface gravity of each planet, moon, and object in the solar system is different. The chart below shows the surface gravity on each planet. Earth has a 1 and is the basis of comparison for all other planets.

Planet	Surface Gravity	Percent
Mercury	0.38	38%
Venus	0.91	91%
Earth	1.00	100%
Mars	0.38	38%
Jupiter	2.36	236%
Saturn	0.92	92%
Uranus	0.89	89%
Neptune	1.12	112%

Planet	Weight (lbs.)
Mercury	_____
Venus	_____
Earth	_____90_____
Mars	_____
Jupiter	_____
Saturn	_____
Uranus	_____
Neptune	_____

1. On which planet would this person weigh the most? Explain why. _____

_____

2. Which two planets have the weakest gravitational pull? Explain why. _____

_____

3. Which planets have more surface gravity than Earth? _____

4. Which planet's surface gravity is the most similar to Earth's? _____

5. If the surface gravity on Earth's moon is 0.17, how much would this person weigh there?

_____

Bill Gates

Directions: Read the passage. Circle the letter beside the best answer to each question below.

Bill Gates was a good student in school, but he was more interested in a new invention. The personal computer was beginning to interest people in the early 1970s, and he was one of these people. By the age of 15, most of his classmates were playing sports and beginning high school. Bill Gates was working with computers. That year, Gates and a classmate, Paul Allen, set up their first software company. They wrote programs for computers. At the age of 20, he and Allen began to design programs to run on PCs. They also started Microsoft® that year. Five years later, Microsoft was chosen by IBM® to design the operating system on their new PC. The operating system is the main program for running a computer's functions.

Bill was not yet 30, and he was running one of the most vital new companies in the world. Gates wrote the system for running the IBM® computer and for similar PCs. His company sold millions of copies. In 1985, Microsoft wrote the first **version** of the Windows® system. It is used on many computers. The company has sold millions of copies of Windows. It is constantly being revised and improved.

Bill Gates is still involved in making his company the leading maker of software for computers. However, he no longer runs the daily operations of his company. He still plans and develops new and better software. The success of his company has made Bill Gates one of the richest men in the world. But he doesn't keep all of his money for himself. He gives a lot to charity. He has created one of the largest charities. This charity supports efforts to improve health, education, and libraries all over the world. Gates has given billions of dollars so people can learn better and live longer.

1. From the context of the passage, what is IBM?

   A. a software company

   B. a PC

   C. a maker of personal computers

   D. a company owned by Gates

2. From the context of the passage, what is the meaning of *version* in the second paragraph?

   A. a form of something

   B. a charity

   C. the final copy of a file

   D. a story

3. What is the operating system of a computer?

   A. the insides of a computer

   B. the main program for controlling a computer's functions

   C. the "on" switch

   D. the maker of software

4. How old was Gates when Microsoft was chosen to develop the operating system for IBM personal computers?

   A. 15   B. 25   C. 30   D. 50

Number Sense

Directions: Read each question about place value and fill in the correct answer circle.

Sample
What is the value of the boldfaced digit?   17.238**9**56

Ⓐ 9 thousandths   Ⓒ 900 thousandths

🅑 9 ten thousandths   Ⓓ 9 millionths

---

1. What is the value of the boldfaced digit?
   437,998,672,009

Ⓐ 30 billion   Ⓒ 30 thousand

Ⓑ 30 million   Ⓓ 30 trillion

5. What is the short word form for 7.7089?

Ⓐ 7 and 7,089 ten thousandths

Ⓑ 7 and 7,089 thousandths

Ⓒ 7 and 7,089 hundred thousandths

Ⓓ 7 and 7,089 hundredths

---

2. What is the value of the boldfaced digit?
   1.098723**9**

Ⓔ 9 millionths   Ⓖ 9 thousandths

Ⓕ 9 billionths   Ⓗ 9 ten millionths

6. Which is equivalent to 0.7?

Ⓔ 0.07

Ⓕ 0.007

Ⓖ 0.70

Ⓗ all of these

---

3. What is the standard form of 209 trillion,
   378 billion, 9 million, 102 thousand, 7?

Ⓐ 209,378,009,102,007

Ⓑ 209,000,009,102,007

Ⓒ 209,378,009,102,700

Ⓓ none of these

7. What is the value of the boldfaced digit?
   8**2**3,607,114,907,429

Ⓐ 2 billion

Ⓑ 20 trillion

Ⓒ 2 trillion

Ⓓ 200 billion

---

4. What is the standard form for eight and
   two thousandths?

Ⓔ 8.2   Ⓖ 8.002

Ⓕ 8.02   Ⓗ 8.0002

8. Which digit is in the ten billions place?
   209,831,000,457,600

Ⓔ 2   Ⓖ 8

Ⓕ 0   Ⓗ 3

Who Lives Where?

Directions: Mike, Anita, Jamal, and Kate live on the same block. Read each clue. Then, mark the chart to see who lives where and in which colored house. Mark an "X" in each box that does not match. Mark an "O" in each box that is a match.

Clues

- Kate's house is farther down the block than Mike's. Neither Kate nor Mike lives in the blue house. Mike doesn't live in the green house.

- Anita does not live third or fourth, and she does not live next to Kate.

- The red house is first on the block, and it is not next to the green house.

- Jamal's house is the last house on the block.

Chart

	1st	2nd	3rd	4th	Red	Blue	Green	Orange
Mike								
Anita								
Jamal								
Kate								
Red								
Blue								
Green								
Orange								

Answers

1. Which house does Mike live in? What color is it? _____

2. Which house does Anita live in? What color is it? _____

3. Which house does Jamal live in? What color is it? _____

4. Which house does Kate live in? What color is it? _____

Summer Reading List

One of the best ways to promote learning and educational growth during summer is through reading. Fortunately, there are a ton of fantastic novels and graphic novels that will interest and delight your middle-school reader. The following is a list of some of those books. Please read the books and/or reviews first to determine if they are appropriate for your child.

If you wish, you can use this chart (and the ones on pages 93-94) to keep you organized. Use the **Dates** column to mark when your child read the book or when it is due back to the library. Use the **Notes** column to remind yourself of what you have read in reviews or of what your child thought of the book after reading it.

Dates	Book Information	Notes
	Fever 1793 by Laurie Halse Anderson In the summer of 1793, Philadelphia was struck with a yellow fever epidemic that killed over 5,000 people. This historical fiction novel tells how 16-year-old Mattie Cook struggled to survive this difficult time.	
	The Unnameables by Ellen Booream Teenager Medford Runyuin lives in a society that only values usefulness. Those who do not conform and follow the rules are banished. Will Medford be able to keep his secret in this modern fantasy tale?	
	All the Broken Pieces by Ann E. Burg After being air-lifted out of Vietnam during the war, 12-year-old Matt struggles with memories of his past in Vietnam and his new life in America with his adopted family.	
	Al Capone Does My Shirts by Gennifer Choldenko In 1935, Moose Flanagan's father gets a job as a prison guard at Alcatraz and moves the entire family to the notorious island. Moose struggles with his new life and the behavior of his autistic sister, but he finds friendship and mischief as well.	
	Walk Two Moons by Sharon Creech When Salamanca Tree Hiddle's mother goes on a spiritual journey and doesn't return, the 13-year-old girl heads off on a road trip with her grandparents to try to find her mother.	
	Mare's War by Tanita S. Davis Octavia and Tali's parents make them go on a cross-country road trip with their grandmother Mare to a family reunion. Along the way, they learn that there is more to their grandmother than meets the eye as she tells them about her youth and her experiences as an African-American in the Women's Army Corps.	
	Johnny Tremain by Esther Forbes Experience the American revolution through the fictional life of Johnny Tremain, a young silversmith apprentice who, after being tragically maimed, finds himself involved in the revolutionary movement.	
	The Diary of Anne Frank by Anne Frank This autobiographical book tells the story of Anne Frank, a young girl hiding from the Nazis during the Holocaust, in her own words.	
	Counting by 7s by Holly Goldberg Sloan With her extreme intelligence and unusual view of the world, 12-year-old Willow Chance has always felt like an outsider. And then she suffers the sudden loss of her adoptive parents. The novel shows how Willow finds love, support, and acceptance in a group of virtual strangers who come together to help a special girl and to find a piece of what they are missing in their own lives.	

Summer Reading List *(cont.)*

Dates	Book Information	Notes
	The Outsiders by S.E. Hinton This modern classic shares the struggles of a group of teenage boys known as the Greasers. Always on the outside, the boys' lives are changed forever when Johnny, a fellow Greaser, kills a rival during a fight.	
	Hattie Big Sky by Kirby Larson Orphaned and alone, 16-year-old Hattie moves from Iowa to Montana to establish her own homestead. She has one year to cultivate her land or she will lose it.	
	The Wreckers by Iain Lawrence This book is the first book in the High Seas Trilogy. It tells the story of 14-year-old John Spence, who is shipwrecked and must elude the local villagers who make their living looting shipwrecked vessels and killing the survivors.	
	White Fang by Jack London *White Fang* is the story of a wild wolf dog who gradually learns to live with humans through a series of often difficult encounters.	
	The Giver by Lois Lowry Jonas has been selected to be the Receiver of Memories, but as he learns the truth about their seemingly perfect society, he learns that a world without poverty, pain, and crime is anything but perfect.	
	Heat by Mike Lupica Michael Arroyo loves baseball and the New York Yankees, but will he lose his big chance to play in the championship game at Yankee Stadium? Will he be able to get his birth certificate from Cuba in time? Will he and his brother be able to avoid social services after the death of their father?	
	Hatchet by Gary Paulsen Brian Robeson is a 13-year-old boy flying to visit his father in the Canadian wilderness when the pilot has a fatal heart attack and the plane crashes into a lake. Brian escapes the wreckage with his life, the clothes on his back, and a hatchet. Now he just has to figure out how to survive.	
	Heart of a Samurai by Margi Preus Manjiro is a young, shipwrecked fisherman who is rescued by an American whaling ship. He decides to go to America with the captain rather than return to Japan. Set in 1841, Manjiro faces distrust, racism, and a clash of cultures.	
	The Westing Game by Ellen Raskin Sixteen people have gathered for the reading of Sam Westing's will, but there is a catch. The will is actually a contest to identify Sam Westing's killer. Can you solve the mystery before they do?	
	Esperanza Rising by Pam Muñoz Ryan Esperanza is used to a life of privilege in Mexico, but when her father is murdered by bandits, her family flees to California to work in the agricultural industry during the 1930s. In the year that follows, Esperanza rises to the challenge as her life and perspective are changed forever.	
	Flygirl by Sherri L. Smith America has joined the fight in WWII, and 18-year-old Ida Mae Jones wants to become a pilot. However, she faces two major obstacles: she's black and a woman.	

Summer Reading List *(cont.)*

Dates	Book Information	Notes
	The Witch of Blackbird Pond by Elizabeth George Speare When Kit Tyler leaves Jamaica to join her aunt and uncle in the puritan colony of Connecticut, she finds it difficult to fit in. Her strange ways and her secret friendship with an old widow lead to trouble. Will she be able to defend herself against accusations of witchcraft?	
	Crash by Jerry Spinelli Can a seventh-grade football player with a long history of being a bully really change? Find out in this anything-but-ordinary book.	
	When You Reach Me by Rebecca Stead Miranda has her world turned upside down when she receives some future-predicting notes. New York City in 1979 is the setting for this mystery.	
	Darkstalker (Wings of Fire: Legends) by Tui T. Sutherland For those who have enjoyed other books in the *Wings of Fire* series, this legendary origin story is a must read. For those who have not, it is still a gripping tale of young dragons blessed (or cursed) with extraordinary gifts and faced with difficult choices that carry vast consequences.	
	Moon Over Manifest by Clare Vanderpool In this Newbery Award-winning novel set during the time of the Great Depression, 12-year-old Abilene is sent for the summer to the town where her father grew up. Manifest, Kansas, feels worn out and washed up, but it holds many secrets. Soon, Abilene and her friends find clues and hunt for meaning in the town's colorful past.	
	Hush by Jacqueline Woodson Toswiah Green's family has to leave their former lives behind and enter the witness protection program after her father witnesses a murder.	

Making the Most of Summertime Reading

When reading these books with your child, you may wish to ask the questions below. The sharing of questions, answers, and ideas will enhance and improve your child's reading comprehension skills. Follow up on short answers to prompt your child to explain their thoughts in greater detail.

- Where does the story take place? How is this setting a "character" in the story?

- When does the story take place? Does it take place in the past, present, or future? Why is this important to the plot?

- Who is a main character in the story? How do the events of the story make this character grow or change as the story goes along?

- Name a minor or supporting character. Why is this character in the story? How do they cause events to occur in the story, and how does this help or hurt the main character?

- Name a conflict in the story. How is it resolved?

- Did any of the events or themes in this story make you think about your own life or examine your own way of thinking? Explain.

Reading Log

This summer my goal is to read _____ books or _____ pages.

Record the books you read below. Give each a rating of 1–5 stars.

Title: _____

Author: _____

Pages: _____

☆☆☆☆☆

Title: _____

Author: _____

Pages: _____

☆☆☆☆☆

Title: _____

Author: _____

Pages: _____

☆☆☆☆☆

Title: _____

Author: _____

Pages: _____

☆☆☆☆☆

Title: _____

Author: _____

Pages: _____

☆☆☆☆☆

Title: _____

Author: _____

Pages: _____

☆☆☆☆☆

Title: _____

Author: _____

Pages: _____

☆☆☆☆☆

Title: _____

Author: _____

Pages: _____

☆☆☆☆☆

Read and Do

Here are some fun ways that your middle-school student can expand on their reading over the summer.

"Like" I Said __/__/__	Use similes to describe characters, settings, or events from the novel. You might even create a few similes to describe your experience of reading the novel. In all, form five similes and explain each.
If It Were Me __/__/__	Imagine that you are stuck in the world of the novel. Which event from the novel would be the most challenging (or enjoyable, frustrating, etc.) for you to deal with? Why?
Déjà Vu __/__/__	Did any of the events from this novel remind you of the events from a different novel or film? Write a paragraph or create a chart comparing the two pieces of art. In your opinion, which one was better? Why?
It's New to Me __/__/__	What one event from the novel's plot (or character, setting, etc.) is something you have never read about in any book before or seen in any film? Write about this element of the book and explain your thoughts about it.
Write to the Author __/__/__	Many authors love to hear from their readers, especially when they hear what people liked best about their books. You can write to an author and send your letter in care of the book's publisher. The publisher's address is listed directly after the title page. Or you may go to the author's website and follow the directions for how to send the author a letter. (To make sure your author is still living, type the author's name into a search engine.)
A Comic Book __/__/__	Turn your favorite book into a comic book. Fold at least two sheets of paper in half and staple them so they make a book. With a ruler and pencil, draw boxes across each page to look like blank comic strips. Then, draw the story of your book as if it were a comic. Draw pictures of your characters and have words coming out of their mouths—just as in a real comic strip.
How I Felt __/__/__	How did this novel make you feel as you read it? Create a page of words, pictures, and colors that you feel describe the mood of the novel.
Write a Sequel __/__/__	What happens to the characters in your book after you finish reading the final page? Why not create a sequel? Will your sequel pick up where the first book left off, or will it take place several months or years after the original book ended?

Book Review

Before they purchase a book online, many people read the reviews written by other readers. In the space provided below, write a review of a book you read. Be sure to support your opinion with at least three specific reasons why you feel that way.

Book Title: _____

Author: _____

Star Rating: ☆ ☆ ☆ ☆ ☆

Review: _____

_____

_____

_____

_____

_____

_____

_____

_____

_____

_____

_____

_____

_____

_____

_____

I **would   would not**   recommend this book to a friend.

Reviewed by: _____

Scientific Process

Use this page to explore the world around you this summer.

I. **State the problem to be solved or investigated.** (What is the purpose of your investigation? What do you hope to prove, demonstrate, or find out?)

_____

II. **Make a hypothesis (scientific guess) suggesting a possible solution to the problem or a plan of investigation.** (What do you think is actually going to happen?)

_____

_____

III. **Test your hypothesis using experimentation, models, and other investigations.** (What experiments will you try? What models are you going to make? What are you actually going to do to test your hypothesis?)

_____

_____

_____

_____

_____

IV. **Record your results.** (Keep an accurate, detailed, and complete record here of what happened in each investigation. Tell what happened and when it happened. Describe any changes and improvements you made. Draw pictures of the model or project.)

_____

_____

_____   Illustration

_____

_____

_____

V. **State your conclusions.** (Tell what you learned.)

_____

_____

Test-Taking Tips

The Secrets to Acing Tests!

- Attend school regularly and be on time.

- Come to school prepared, rested, and ready to learn.

- Complete all of your classroom and homework assignments.

- Ask for help if you don't understand.

- Spend time every day studying and reviewing material.

- Create an organized and quiet place in which to study.

- Know that procrastination is the enemy of achievement!

Multiple-Choice Strategies

1. Read the question or phrase (stem) carefully.

2. Cover the options and make a prediction.

3. If your prediction or something close to it appears, select it.

4. If your prediction does not appear, read each option carefully.

5. Eliminate any silly options.

6. Eliminate any options you know to be incorrect.

7. A stem and option that create a grammatically incorrect statement may be an indication that it is wrong.

8. Preface the stem and option choice with the phrase "It is true that. . ." If the stem and option create a true statement, it is an indication that it is correct.

9. If "All of the above" is an option and at least two of the other options are correct, then select "All of the above."

10. If "All of the above" is an option and you know that at least one of the options is wrong, then eliminate both "All of the above" and the other incorrect option.

11. If "None of the above" is an option and at least one of the options is correct, then eliminate "None of the above" as a possibility.

Tough to Spell

Below and on page 101 are some of the most commonly misspelled words in the English language. Practice spelling each word, then use this list to remind you how these words are spelled.

accept _____

advice _____

believe _____

calendar _____

changeable _____

collectible _____

congratulations _____

conscience _____

definitely _____

dictionary _____

embarrass _____

excellence _____

experience _____

explanation _____

fascinating _____

February _____

finally _____

foreign _____

grateful _____

guarantee _____

happily _____

harass _____

height _____

heroes _____

humor _____

independent _____

intelligence _____

judgment _____

length _____

library _____

lightning _____

marshmallow _____

miniature _____

mischievous _____

misspell _____

naturally _____

Tough to Spell *(cont.)*

necessary _____

neighbor _____

noticeable _____

occasionally _____

opinion _____

opportunity _____

personal _____

piece _____

possession _____

prejudice _____

privilege _____

realize _____

really _____

receive _____

receipt _____

recommend _____

refrigerator _____

rhythm _____

sentence _____

separate _____

similar _____

success _____

temperature _____

tomorrow _____

truly _____

twelfth _____

unique _____

until _____

usually _____

vacuum _____

valuable _____

visible _____

weather _____

Wednesday _____

weird _____

writing _____

Proofreading Marks

Editor's Mark	Meaning	Example
≡	capitalize	they fished in lake tahoe.
/	make it lowercase	Five Students missed the Bus.
sp.	spelling mistake	The day was clowdy and cold.
⊙	add a period	Tomorrow is a holiday⊙
ℒ	delete (remove)	One person knew the the answer.
∧	add a word	Six were in the litter.
⌃,	add a comma	He planted peas corn, and squash.
∿	reverse words or letters	An otter swam in the bed kelp.
⌄'	add an apostrophe	The child's bike was blue.
⌄" ⌄"	add quotation marks	Why can't I go? she cried.
#	make a space	He ate two red apples.
⌣	close the space	Her favorite game is soft ball.
¶	begin a new paragraph	to know. Next on the list

Measurement

U.S. Customary Units

Length/Distance

12 inches	=	1 foot
3 feet	=	1 yard
5,280 feet	=	1 mile
1,760 yards	=	1 mile

Volume

3 teaspoons	=	1 tablespoon
8 ounces	=	1 cup
2 cups	=	1 pint
4 cups	=	1 quart
2 pints	=	1 quart
16 cups	=	1 gallon
8 pints	=	1 gallon
4 quarts	=	1 gallon

Mass

16 ounces	=	1 pound
2,000 pounds	=	1 short ton

Metric Units

Length/Distance

10 millimeters	=	1 centimeter
1,000 millimeters	=	1 meter
100 centimeters	=	1 meter
1,000 meters	=	1 kilometer

Volume

1,000 milliliters	=	1 liter
1,000 liters	=	1 kiloliter

Mass

1,000 milligrams	=	1 gram
1,000 grams	=	1 kilogram

Answer Key

Page 12

1. 57,343
2. 288,184
3. 4,722,070
4. 3,542,130
5. 17,710,528
6. 51,298,965
7. 26,896,941
8. 196,493,054

9. 2,804
10. 1,927
11. 1,223
12. 643
13. 32
14. 1,396
15. 552
16. 124,000

Page 13

1. B   2. D   3. C   4.   D

Page 14

Descriptions may vary.

1. *atmosphere*—the gaseous layer that surrounds Earth
2. *hydrosphere*—the layer of water on Earth
3. *lithosphere*—this layer includes Earth's crust and the upper mantle; it is hard and rocky
4. *mantle*—this layer is semi-solid and hot
5. *core*—the center of Earth is very dense and extremely hot; it consists of the inner core, which is solid, and the outer core, which is liquid

Page 15

Answers may vary. Possible answers include:

1. Molly bought groceries, and she also bought flowers.
2. Tracy swims every day, and she also jogs three miles.
3. Hawaii is a state now, but it was not one until 1959.
4. Tomorrow is a national holiday, so schools and banks will be closed.
5. The singer's voice was tired, but she didn't cancel the concert.
6. We visited St. Louis, but we did not go inside the Gateway Arch.
7. My dog loves the forest. He runs all over, sniffing trees.
8. The girl painted a picture, and she hoped to give it to her mother.
9. She loves hot chocolate, so she drinks three cups a day.
10. The soccer team won the match, and they earned a trophy.
11. A bird made a nest in Mark's chimney, so he had to call a chimney sweep.
12. Grandpa taught me to fish, and we caught three trout.
13. Honeybees have a hive in that tree, so don't get stung.
14. She trained hard for four years, and her hard work paid off.
15. The photographer took many photos, but we never saw them.

Page 16

1. 3,200 feet
2. 40 minutes
3. 10,000 feet
4. 7,128 feet
5. 396 minutes

6. 7,740 feet
7. 24,000 feet
8. 503 minutes
9. 410 minutes
10. 30,400 feet

Page 17

1. fact
2. opinion
3. opinion
4. fact
5. fact

6. opinion
7. opinion
8. opinion
9. opinion
10. fact

11. opinion
12. fact
13. fact
14. opinion
15. fact

Page 19

Africa: Egypt, Libya, Algeria, Morocco, Ethiopia, Sudan, Kenya, Nigeria, Tanzania, Angola

Asia: China, Japan, India, Vietnam, Iran, Saudi Arabia, Philippines, Israel, Iraq, Thailand

Europe: United Kingdom, France, Germany, Spain, Italy, Greece, Sweden, Switzerland, Poland, Hungary, Ireland

Answer Key *(cont.)*

Page 19 *(cont.)*

North America: Canada, United States, Mexico, Cuba, Costa Rica, Nicaragua, Panama, El Salvador, Guatemala

South America: Brazil, Uruguay, Argentina, Chile, Bolivia, Peru, Ecuador, Colombia, Venezuela, Paraguay

Page 20

1. B   3. D   5. C   7. B
2. G   4. F   6. E   8. H

Page 21

The final answer should be the month, day, and year of the student's birthday.

Page 22

1. 16   8. 2
2. 2   9. 12 cups
3. 128   10. 64 fluid ounces
4. 4   11. 20 quarts
5. 6   12. 18 cups
6. 3   13. 24 pints
7. 16   14. 4 gallons

Page 23

1. All farmers <u>who are growing the new hybrid of wheat</u> are expected to have a good harvest.
2. Kareem Abdul-Jabbar, <u>who holds several NBA records</u>, retired from basketball in 1989.
3. <u>Founded in 1636</u>, Harvard College is the oldest college in the United States.
4. The inventions <u>created by Thomas Edison</u> have changed the way people live around the world.
5. Jose has a tremendous fear of spiders, <u>which is known as arachnophobia</u>.
6. The championship cup, <u>dusty and filled with coins</u>, sat on the highest shelf.

Page 24

5, 4, 2, 7, 1, 6, 3

Page 25

1. they believed that a person needed their body in the afterlife
2. 70
3. canopic jars
4. embalmers
5. what ancient Egyptians ate and what kinds of diseases they suffered from

Page 26

1. $\frac{13}{30}$ 5. $1\frac{1}{3}$ 9. $3\frac{41}{42}$ 13. $\frac{16}{81}$
2. $\frac{7}{20}$ 6. $9\frac{3}{28}$ 10. $7\frac{1}{30}$ 14. $8\frac{1}{12}$
3. $\frac{3}{4}$ 7. $\frac{8}{9}$ 11. $13\frac{1}{35}$ 15. $\frac{35}{54}$
4. $11\frac{27}{35}$ 8. $\frac{11}{18}$ 12. $5\frac{1}{12}$ 16. $1\frac{3}{5}$

Page 28

1. asteroid belt   5. asteroid
2. solar system   6. meteorite
3. tail   7. meteor
4. Meteoroids

Page 29

1. B   3. A   5. F
2. D   4. C   6. E
7. elude
8. conveyance
9. malevolent
10. rambles
11. feckless
12. denizen

Page 30

1. C   3. D   5. A   7. B
2. E   4. H   6. F   8. H

Page 31

1. fat cat   7. quick chick
2. book crook   8. spud bud
3. grape ape   9. jacket racket
4. dime lime   10. wider spider
5. best nest   11. sandy candy
6. weird beard   12. snake brake

Page 32

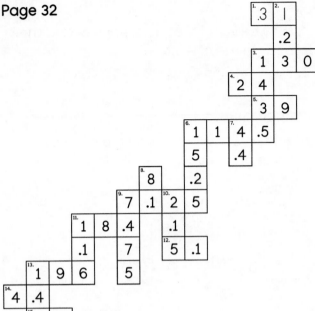

Page 33

1. C   2. A   3. C

Page 34

1. A
2. O
3. 2 out of 4; 50%

4.

FF	Ff
fF	ff

5. 1 out of 4; 25%

Page 35

1. "Are you going to take the trash out?" Mom asked David.
2. David yawned. "I'm busy playing video games," he said.
3. "It won't take itself out," Mom reminded him.
4. "I'll do it!" David exclaimed.
5. "He'll forget until tonight," Mom muttered to the dog.

6. "Woof!" barked the dog, sniffing the trash can.
7. "David!" yelled Mom. "Take out this trash now!"
8. "Okay, okay," said David. "I'm turning off the game."
9. He took out the trash. "It stinks," he said.
10. "I'm finished," he told Mother. "Can I have my allowance?"

Page 36

1. $45.00 (3%)
2. $1,545.00
3. $0
4. $0
5. Lee didn't earn any interest because the balance was not high enough to qualify for interest.
6. $3.50 (1%)
7. $353.50
8. $294.00 (3%)
9. $10,094.00
10. $353.29 (3.5%)

Page 37

1. composed
2. permanent
3. personalized
4. recede
5. grueling
6. simultaneous
7. contributes
8. priceless
9. infuriating
10. overwhelmed
11. conform
12. random

Page 39

1. 21 + 22 = 43
2. 43 + 19 = 62
3. 62 − 25 = 37
4. 37 + 24 = 61
5. 61 − 23 = 38
6. 38 + 18 = 56
7. 56 + 20 = 76
8. 76 − 26 = 50

Page 40

1. B   2. G   3. A   4. G

Answer Key (cont.)

Page 41

4	5	9	8	6	2	1	3	7
2	8	6	1	3	7	5	9	4
7	1	3	5	9	4	8	6	2
5	9	2	6	7	8	3	4	1
8	6	7	3	4	1	9	2	5
1	3	4	9	2	5	6	7	8
3	4	5	2	8	9	7	1	6
9	2	8	7	1	6	4	5	3
6	7	1	4	5	3	2	8	9

Page 42

1. Mean: 27; Median: 18.5; Mode: 17
2. Mean: 232.5; Median: 214; Modes: 108, 229
3. Mean: 11.2; Median: 10; Mode: 8
4. Mean: 1,542; Median: 1,277; Mode: 1,872
5. Mean: 36; Median: 32.5; Mode: 49.5

Page 43

1. taught, cite
2. taut, peak
3. peek, presents, allowed
4. lesson, passed
5. presence, aloud
6. accept, past
7. site, except
8. effect, lessen, affect

Page 44

Answers will vary, but Lena is a newspaper reporter.

Page 45

1. D
2. K
3. G
4. M
5. B
6. F
7. O
8. I
9. C
10. J
11. N
12. H
13. L
14. E
15. A
16. Mount Olympus
17. the Olympic Games

Page 46

1. 75%   3. 75%   5. 75%   7. 64%   9. 70%
2. 72%   4. 60%   6. 80%   8. 60%   10. 75%

Page 48

1. K   3. A   5. B   7. E   9. C   11. F
2. I   4. G   6. J   8. D   10. H
12. circulatory   16. skeletal
13. nervous   17. excretory
14. endocrine   18. digestive
15. integumentary

Page 49

1. G   3. E   5. B   7. A   9. C
2. F   4. H   6. D   8. I
10. ophthalmologist   14. mineralogist
11. neonatologist   15. psychologist
12. criminologist   16. etymologist
13. ornithologist   17. histologist

Page 50

1. C   3. A   5. B   7. A
2. H   4. F   6. H   8. H

Page 51

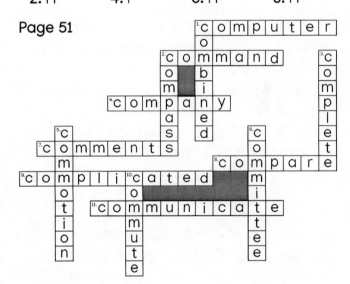

Page 52

Part 1
2. 4,782,969
3. 50,625
4. 100,000,000
5. 46,656
6. 81

Part 2
1. 6^5; 7,776
2. 7^3; 343
3. 2^4; 16
4. 11^5; 161,051

Answer Key *(cont.)*

Page 53

1. A 2. B 3. C

Page 54

3. berries, grasshopper, lizard
4. grass, antelope, lion
5. water plants, snail, duck, great-horned owl
6. small plants, moose, wolf, vulture
7. bark, hare, mink, great-horned owl
8. plankton, clams, sea lions, great white shark

Page 55

1. You're (or You are) the first one in your family to have a bicycle of your very own.
2. Jane Smith, Kim Choi, and Sitara Jaworski went to Lakewood Mall to buy new clothes.
3. (correct)
4. They were the very last ones to leave the room on Valentine's Day.
5. Are you the heir to your wealthy uncle's estate?
6. We don't (or do not) want to go to the party later.
7. Jerry had his paper with him, but he didn't (or did not) have his pencil.
8. Ari is never (or isn't ever) going shopping with those girls again.
9. There are hardly any differences between the three girls.
10. On Independence Day, we went to the Colorado River with our friends.
11. "Hurry, hurry!" Mother yelled. "I need help with these (or those, the) groceries."
12. (correct)

Page 56

1. 4	5. 8	9. 29	13. 45
2. 70	6. 17	10. 6	14. 90
3. 13	7. 5	11. 15	15. 700
4. 20	8. 19	12. 50	16. 62

Page 57

1. genres
2. Science fiction is based on scientific discoveries; fantasy has supernatural elements.
3. science fiction
4. fantasy

Page 59

1. promote	5. justice	9. establish
2. secure	6. welfare	10. defense
3. insure	7. ordain	11. domestic
4. union	8. posterity	12. tranquility

Page 60

1. D	4. A	7. A	10. D
2. C	5. C	8. C	11. B
3. E	6. B	9. E	12. E

Page 61

The youngest child's name is Cathy!

Page 62

1. –58	6. –96	11. 49	16. 28
2. –13	7. 67	12. 120	17. –7
3. 0	8. –10	13. –56	18. –6
4. 40	9. –20	14. –126	19. –56
5. –36	10. –11	15. 3	20. 12

Page 63

1. positive, negative 4. negative, positive
2. positive, negative 5. positive, negative
3. negative, positive 6. positive, negative

Page 64

1. The Statue of Liberty
2. mild eyes, silent lips, mighty woman, beacon hand
3. brazen—marked by contemptuous boldness
   beacon—signal for guidance
   astride—with one leg on each side
   yearning—to feel a longing or a craving
4. tired, yearning to be free, homeless, tempest-tost, huddled masses, poor

Answer Key *(cont.)*

Page 65

Answers will vary, but should be similar to the following:

- *Executive Branch*—makes sure that the laws of the United States are obeyed. The president is the head of the Executive branch and commander-in-chief of the military.
- *Legislative Branch*—has the power to make laws. The Congress has two parts: the House of Representatives and the Senate.
- *Judicial Branch*—interprets and applies the laws. It consists of the court system, including the Supreme Court, which is the highest court in the land.

Page 66

Page 68

Answers will vary, but should be similar to the following:

- Renewable energy sources are unlimited or can be easily replaced.
- Nonrenewable energy sources are limited or hard to replace.

1. renewable   3. nonrenewable
2. renewable   4. nonrenewable

Page 69

1. no	4. yes	7. yes	10. yes	13. no
2. yes	5. no	8. yes	11. yes	14. no
3. yes	6. yes	9. no	12. no	

Page 70

1. B	3. C	5. D	7. A
2. G	4. G	6. H	8. H

Page 71

1. TO FLY MUST BE A WONDERFUL FEELING!
2. HAVING AMBITION IS HALF THE BATTLE!
3. IF YOU GET LOST, THERE IS NOTHING LEFT TO DO BUT ASK FOR DIRECTIONS.

Page 72

1. 1960
2. 1990 and 2000
3. 1960
4. 1950–1960
5. 1990 and 2000
6. 1970–1980
7. 1960–1970
8. 10 and 11
9. 12 and 13
10. 16
11. 7, 8, 9
12. taller
13. 14

Page 73

1. a   2. c   3. c

Page 74

1. d   2. b   3. d   4. d

Page 75

1. Frida Kahlo was a famous artist; she lived in Mexico and painted pictures.
2. I'm Kellie's best friend; she always invites me to her birthday parties.
3. not related
4. Pablo cannot stop coughing; his father has gone to buy cough syrup.
5. Some say to apply butter to a burned area on the body; this is not a good idea.
6. not related
7. When handling the American flag, never let it touch the ground; this shows respect for the flag.
8. not related
9. Richard Bach wrote about seagulls; later, he wrote about airplanes.
10. *Metamorphosis* is a book by Franz Kafka; it's about a man who turns into a bug.
11. Chickens make wonderful pets; they'll even come when you call them.
12. Driving on Route 66 is exciting; you never know what you'll see.
13. The wedding was postponed; the bride and groom were ill with the flu.
14. They put their house up for sale; they're moving to Alaska.

Page 76

1. 31.4 ft.   6. 47.1 cm
2. 125.6 cm   7. 113.04 ft.
3. 43.96 ft.   8. 125.6 yd.
4. 69.08 in.   9. 100.48 m
5. 25.12 m   10. 502.4 mm

Page 77

1. C   2. B   3. A   4. F   5. D   6. E
7. sentinel   10. lunge
8. irks   11. ornery
9. caper   12. protrude

Page 79

```
D  E (A  I  N  A  V  L  Y  S  N  N  E  P)
(C  N  E  W  H  A  M  P  S  H  I  R  E) L
 A  O  W (R  H  O  D  E  I  S  L  A  N  D)
 A  A  N  I  L  O  R  A  C  H  T  R  O  N
 R  E  L  N  I  A  V (G  E  O  R  G  I  A)
(N  E  W  J  E  R  S  E  Y) P  H  O  U  L
(S  O  U  T  H  C  A  R  O  L  I  N  A) Y
 R  G  N  I  R  A  T  M  S  P  N  A  L  R
 M  Z  C  A  I  R (V  I  R  G  I  N  I  A)
 W (S  T  T  E  S  U  H  C  A  S  S  A  M)
 L  E  C  W  E  D  F  N  E  U  L  R  G  I
 I  J (K  R  O  Y  W  E  N) W  T  K  U  A
```

13th: Rhode Island   6th: Massachusetts
12th: North Carolina   5th: Connecticut
11th: New York   4th: Georgia
10th: Virginia   3rd: New Jersey
9th: New Hampshire   2nd: Pennsylvania
8th: South Carolina   1st: Delaware
7th: Maryland

Page 80

1. B   3. D   5. A   7. C
2. G   4. G   6. H   8. E

Page 81

2. Old Woman Who Lived in a Shoe
3. Goldilocks and the Three Bears
4. The Itsy Bitsy Spider
5. Hey Diddle Diddle, the Cat and the Fiddle
6. Three Blind Mice
7. Old MacDonald Had a Farm
8. Sleeping Beauty

Answer Key (cont.)

Page 82

1. 45°	4. 30°	7. 90°	10. 130°
2. 60°	5. 40°	8. 60°	11. 120°
3. 70°	6. 100°	9. 100°	12. 55°

Page 83

1. affect
2. beside
3. accept
4. counsel
5. farther
6. proceed
7. principal
8. advice
9. aisle
10. allot
11. loose
12. latter
13. morale
14. Who's

Page 85

1. b   2. d   3. a

Page 86

1. A and B
   C and D
   E and F
   G and H
   A and C
   B and D
   E and G
   F and H

4. I and J
   K and L
   M and N
   O and P
   J and L
   N and P
   I and K
   M and O

2. B and F
   D and H
   A and E
   C and G

5. J and N
   L and P
   I and M
   K and O

3. A = 150°
   B = 30°
   C = 30°
   D = 150°
   E = 150°
   F = 30°
   G = 30°
   H = 150°

6. I = 30°
   J = 150°
   K = 150°
   L = 30°
   M = 30°
   N = 150°
   O = 150°
   P = 30°

Page 88

Planet	Weight (lbs.)
Mercury	34.2
Venus	81.9
Earth	90
Mars	34.2
Jupiter	212.4
Saturn	82.8
Uranus	80.1
Neptune	100.8

1. Jupiter, because it has the greatest mass and strongest gravitational pull
2. Mercury and Mars, because they have the smallest amounts of mass
3. Jupiter and Neptune
4. Saturn
5. 15.3 pounds

Page 89

1. C   2. A   3. B   4. B

Page 90

1. A	3. A	5. A	7. B
2. H	4. G	6. G	8. H

Page 91

	1st	2nd	3rd	4th	Red	Blue	Green	Orange
Mike	X	O	X	X	X	X	X	O
Anita	O	X	X	X	O	X	X	X
Jamal	X	X	X	O	X	O	X	X
Kate	X	X	O	X	X	X	O	X
Red	O	X	X	X				
Blue	X	X	X	O				
Green	X	X	O	X				
Orange	X	O	X	X				

1. 2nd house, orange
2. 1st house, red
3. 4th house, blue
4. 3rd house, green

Reward Chart